JIM CROW:

A POSTMORTEM
POLITICAL ANALYSIS

Michael E. Orok, Ph.D.

authorHOUSE®

AuthorHouse™
1663 Liberty Drive
Bloomington, IN 47403
www.authorhouse.com
Phone: 1-800-839-8640

Published by AuthorHouse   10/13/2014

ISBN: 978-1-4969-1807-9 (sc)
ISBN: 978-1-4969-1808-6 (hc)
ISBN: 978-1-4969-1806-2 (e)

To my mother Cornelia, who always believed in me and encouraged me to push forward despite all odds.

Contents

Preface

This book was inspired by research projects undertaken in America and my personal observations over a period of ten years about my frustration regarding the condition of African American life. As an immigrant from Africa who knew very little about the *Brown v. Board of Education* lawsuit and explicit Jim Crow laws, I was blindsided by the tremendous amount of prejudice and racism in the United States during the post-Civil Rights era. I immigrated to the United States in the late 1970s and, fortunately, gained admission into a historically Black university, Central State University in Ohio. There I had the advantage of learning about African American life in a racially tolerant and dynamic environment. I was sheltered from overt racism but exposed to self-imposed restrictions and institutionalized constructs that were almost by design a derailment of any positive thoughts and/or orientations I had regarding the struggles of African Americans in a country considered the most influential and powerful in the world. In many instances, I was antagonized and discriminated against by trusted comrades, but I was determined to seek the truth about the foundation of such prejudices.

After more than a decade of intellectual dialogue, uninterrupted scholarship, and intense participation in African American life, I felt prepared to put my thoughts and experiences on paper and perhaps define what I consider the undergirding truth, negative images, and psychological underpinnings that attempt to wreak havoc in the lives of many African Americans.

The journey has not been easy. I graduated from Central State University with an increased appreciation for what I define as "Black plight" and struggle with my thoughts shaped by such history professors as Dr. Joseph Lewis. But I needed a different perspective, and comparative documentation, which were only achieved after graduation with a graduate degree from a predominantly White institution.

To ground my intellectual development and experiences, I sought knowledge from whence the masters arose. I arrived at Atlanta University in Atlanta, Georgia, birthplace of the Civil Rights movement, considered the self-proclaimed "Black Mecca." The university was founded by Dr. W. E. B. Du Bois, who explicitly and painfully described the "souls of Black folk" in his groundbreaking work in 1903. The Atlanta University Center was and still is a rich, intellectual environment, a cluster of seven historically Black universities, the largest center of Black learning in the world. I believed, at that juncture, I had almost literally arrived home. As a political science graduate student pursuing a doctoral degree, my learning intensified. I was motivated by the dearth of scholarship about world outlook that was easily accessible at the center. I met individuals with multiple attitudes and contemporary theories about racism and prejudice. The lines between empirical and qualitative research were blurred; learning about racism, prejudice, discrimination, and emerging research assumed a psychological discourse. Experiences crystallized, and scholars were able to propose varied research paradigms for understanding prejudice, racism, desegregation, and other social practices without fear of isolation by mainstream scholarship. At this point, I began the arduous task of accumulating several years of work in the field via research-based experiences, hoping one day I would have the opportunity to offer some evaluation of African American life based on personal experiences and perhaps contemporary scholarship.

This work is an attempt aimed at documenting some historical antecedents that weave together the complex reality of African American life in the United States. This phenomenological work utilizes a descriptive approach to document and demonstrate the many tenets of American political life, with special emphasis on racial turbulence and inequalities as they become a historically significant dominant culture. This work also includes contemporary discourse that sheds some light on how far America has come racially and any prognoses for the future based on the evidence in the literature. While the material is inconclusive, it serves as a spatial utilization of past research information and life experiences with cumulative literature aimed at adding to the discourse about issues relating to African American life. It is expected to enrich the scholarship in African American and minority studies in the United States. I am thankful to Central State University (Ohio), Atlanta University (Clark-Atlanta), and Albany State University for assisting me in shaping my thoughts regarding African American life and struggles in twenty-first-century America.

Acknowledgments

This book has been contemplated over the past few years. Each time I summed up the determination and courage to complete it, I was faced with other life challenges. But with the comforting and enduring spirit of the Almighty God, I persisted, and now I can say it is finally done.

I would like to express my gratitude to the many professional colleagues who always thought I should complete the book and indicated their eagerness to read it. I particularly thank my wife, Dr. Teresa Merriweather Orok, who I consider to be my "greatest cheerleader," and my very perceptive, determined, and visionary daughter, Ekemini, for their understanding—especially during those times when I did not feel like talking because I was buried in thought about what I would write in the next chapter.

I also thank Stashia Bryant Emanuel, who worked with me on revising the chapters and providing some input. I am indebted to Ms. P. Cameron of the department of public administration at Tennessee State University, who came to my rescue and retyped the entire manuscript after I had lost my original. To the late John Perdue in Albany, Georgia, who assisted me in developing the concept for this book, and to Carolyn Mansfield, my former administrative assistant at Albany State University in Georgia, I say thanks for all your comments and support.

I also thank all of those who read, wrote, offered comments, and assisted in the editing, proofreading, and design, especially the staff of AuthorHouse Publishing.

Introduction

During the 1930s, after thousands of African Americans had been put to death by mobs—particularly in the South—"lynchings were no longer unusual or shocking events. Approximately 4,742 individuals were lynched between 1882 and 1968; of the victims, 3,445, or 73 percent, were Black. During the heyday of lynchings (1889 to 1928), 3,224 individuals were lynched, of whom 2,522 (78 percent) were Black. Typically, the victims were hanged or burned to death by mobs of White vigilantes, frequently in front of thousands of spectators, many of whom would take pieces of the dead person's body as souvenirs to help remember the spectacular event."[1]

During the twentieth century, there were three major responses within the Black intellectual community to the "predicament" of being Black in America. All three were born during the first half of the twentieth century but continued to attract political academic adherents in the second half as well, albeit in transformed fashion.

Marcus Garvey's Back-to-Africa Movement and Black Nationalism were based on the premise that struggle of racial equality was futile, given the deep-rooted racism of White America. He believed political and cultural independence and, ultimately, prosperity could be achieved only through a wholesale return to the African motherland. Closely allied to this movement, at least in philosophy, was the Black Muslim movement led by Elijah Muhammad, who advocated rejection of the White world in favor of economic development within the Black community and cultural nationalism.

W. E. B. Du Bois, a founder of the Niagara Movement (a precursor of the NAACP), advocated that Blacks fight for equality within the majority community. This became the predominant strategy of the 1960s Civil Rights Movement, although it took a variety of forms

---

[1] Richard M. Perloff (2000). "The Press and Lynchings of African Americans," *Journal of Black Studies,* Ohio: Cleveland State University, January, 315-30; see also Brundage, W. F. (1993). "Lynching in the New South: Georgia and Virginia, 1880–1930," Urbana: University of Illinois Press.

ranging from sit-ins to voter registration drives to nationally publicized protest demonstrations to local actions.

Booker T. Washington, founder of Tuskegee Institute, promoted the ideal of self-improvement for Blacks within a segregated system. All of these strategies were designed as a means toward an end. African Americans were in search of a common successful agenda that would minimize White racism and curtail "Jim Crowism." This agenda involved the development and implementation of a caste system practiced in the late 1800s and mid-1960s in the United States. This caste system consisted of anti-Black laws designed to prevent Blacks from participating in the American political system or in influencing political decision-making. The practice of segregation by Whites was not conditioned by the need to properly address Black problems; segregation became an indefensible approach designed to motivate "racial antipathy."[2]

In fact, in 1949, Gordon Allport defined prejudice in psychological terms, and in an attempt to identify prejudicial attitudes from expressions, he arrived at the same conclusion. In both cases, attitudes and expressions yielded potential racial labels. It appears then that while Whites were utilizing "Jim Crow" psychological games through the structural implementation of laws that limited African American participation movement and access, African Americans utilized psychological attitudes and actions that sought corrective measures through antagonizing economic, cultural, and historical systems. It is instructive to point out that when using the above analysis to describe African American response to racism, it clearly debunks the notion that African Americans were stereotypically and explicitly violent in their search for social balance.[3]

Often the question "What do Black folks want?" is asked. Those who pose this question evidently do not understand group dynamics in America, especially as they impact everyday living.

---

[2]   Anthony Rice. "A Legacy Transformed: The Christiana Riot in Historical Memory" (2012). Theses and dissertations paper 1985. This dissertation is brought to you for free and open access by Lehigh Preserve. It has been accepted for inclusion in *Theses and Dissertations* by an authorized administrator of Lehigh Preserve. For more information, please contact preserve@lehigh.edu.

[3]   G.W. Allport (1958). *The Nature of Prejudice* (abridged), Garden City, NJ: Doubleday.

African American children grow up on an unleveled playing field; therefore, their response to social discourse and phenomena is shaped by historical and psychological experiences. Many social psychologists posit that the primary reason individuals respond to this and similar questions in a hostile (or racist) way can be blamed on a behavior that is grounded in years of training based on their life experiences; a life lived every day in their social setting draw the following underlying observations:

> Despite vast changes in attitudes toward Blacks in America today, most social scientists are in agreement that even through blatant and extreme forms of racism against African Americans are now relegated to the past, more subtle and indirect forms of racism remain. In particular, research has not focused on the principle, implementation gap, or the apparent contradiction between White Americans expressed support for the principle of racial equality and their consistent opposition to the implementation of any concrete policies that might actually promote racial equality in practice. (Sidanus and Pratto, May 2001, Modern Racism theories)[4]

Clearly, then, there is the issue of submissive and dominant groups where the dominant group refuses to accept the legitimacy of the other, seeking only submission from it. Humans have a general desire for social identification based on positive attributes, and acceptable and justifiable relations. African Americans are not different in this regard. History has judged the African American negatively with unjustifiable stereotypes; therefore, any attempt to introduce discipline into the range of relationships is seen as perpetuating inequality and in many cases outright psychological desegregation and racial bias.

In ensuing chapters, we will attempt to document some historical antecedents that weave the complex reality of African American life

---

[4]   The citation is drawn from a very impressive work on racial inequality in the United States by Jim Sidaniuis and Felicia Pratto titled "Social Dominance: An Intergroup Theory of Social Hierarchy and Oppression," United Kingdom: Press Syndicate, Cambridge University, 2001, 16.

in the United States. The reader is cautioned that what is presented is by no means conclusive; it is a spatial utilization of past research and life experiences with cumulative literature aimed at adding to the discourse about issues relating to African American life. No discussion about inequality, racism, segregation, and prejudice is complete until all vestiges of social and economics domination and discrimination have been eliminated. We will enter a new and demanding chapter in African American life. A new historical chapter will unfold, and scholars will scramble to fill in the pages of history.

Chapter 1

POSTWAR BOOM TIMES

We are now concerned with the peace of the world.—George Marshall

In the development of the United States, several major political events contributed to the shaping of the nation. However, none would change the course of history so rapidly as the end of the Second World War. In August 1945, President Harry S. Truman ordered the use of atomic bombs, which were dropped on the Japanese cities or Hiroshima and Nagasaki. The resulting Japanese and German surrender led to an enormous economic setback. With the end of World War II, the United States assumed the inevitable position of being the only country that emerged from the war with a stable economy and a measurable means of production.[5]

While the end of war was a welcome opportunity for world peace and peaceful coexistence, at home it was a mixed blessing. The economic programs of the New Deal era of the 1930s placed tremendous responsibility on the government of economic development and stability. The government had difficulties resolving unemployment, especially after the sudden demobilization of more than ten million soldiers. The country was not in a state of flux and the U.S. Congress was forced to set in place several strategic economic initiatives aimed at abating further hemorrhaging of the economy and the possibility of economic depression.

Among these initiatives was the passage of the Servicemen's Readjustment Act of 1944 (popularly called the GI Bill of Rights), which provided education, insurance, and other benefits to former soldiers. The Employment Act of 1946 promised the employment of a large number of Americans but not full employment; policymakers in government knew a promise of full employment for all citizens would risk the introduction of socialist tendencies into the American free-enterprise system.

---

[5]   Robert H. Ferrell (1980). *Off the Record: The Private Papers of Harry S. Truman,* New York: Harper and Row, 55–6.

Even though the economic system was still intact, key aspects of the machinery for progress were dwindling. For example, manufacturing jobs had fallen near record lows due to corporate mergers. This prompted Congress to establish the Small Business Administration in 1953.

According to Dave Elder, Assemblyman, D-San Pedro, "The national debt in 1945 was $260 billion and the gross national product (GNP) reached $212 billion. In other words, our national debt was just over 22% greater than our GNP. In comparison, the national debt for 1991 is estimated to be $3,617 billion, versus a GNP of $5,616 billion. Our current estimated national debt is 36% smaller than our GNP, or about half what it was in 1945 in relative terms.[6] But even with this staggeringly negative economic news, other areas of the economy were booming. College enrollment increased, and the nation witnessed great population shifts through an increase in marriages.

But while the military was integrated with the passage of the GI Bill, one element in American life was left unaddressed. What would become of the African American servicemen who fought side by side with their White counterparts after the war, knowing that at home, Jim Crow laws were still in effect? Would they and other African American non-military persons receive the same benefits as Whites and participate in nation building? It is clear that while the government was busy nation-building, it ignored this social dynamics that would eventually cause a sociopolitical, economic, and psychological breakdown of the American social milieu, a setback that would not be resolved even after fifty years.

During the decade following the end of the Second World War, much of the nation's attention was directed at economic expansion, as urban areas swelled with increasing numbers of immigrants from small towns and farm areas north and south.

Nationally, there seemed to be a tacit agreement between Southern political leaders (virtually all nominally Democratic but conservative) and northern Republicans and Democrats that segregation would not

---

[6]   Dave Elder. "Dealing with National Debt," *Los Angeles Times,* January 21, 1992.

become a national issue. A notable exception to this was the desegregation of the armed forces, ordered by President Truman in 1948.[7]

Just as slavery was tolerated by most national officials for two centuries before the Civil War, the pervasive racial caste system in the South and its ugly byproducts, such as lynchings, were only in exceptional cases a part of the national dialogue. Segregation in northern cities, especially in Chicago and Boston (as they were expressed in housing patterns and the drawing of school district borders), expanded under cover of unwritten and rarely challenged practices among real estate brokers and school administrators.

On the personal level, paternalism helped perpetuate the Jim Crow system. White employers and Black employees had personal relationships, which sometimes extended through generations and softened the edges of an inherently cruel way of life. A Black maid might work for a family for decades, raising the White family's children, participating in their lives in an intimate, albeit subservient way. The meager wages, typically $10 a week, often for sixty hours' work, were often supplemented by hand-me-down clothes and leftover food for the maid's family. If the maid or one of her family fell ill, the White employers might well arrange and even pay for medical care.

The small rewards of paternalistic relationships between Whites and Blacks, based as they were on dramatic inequality, came with a price: inequality had to be accepted without question or the servant could become unemployed, homeless, or worse. In a small town, a White family used to arranging good outcomes for a Black servant could just as easily arrange a disastrous outcome for someone who dared defy or even criticize White supremacy. All the weapons of power and coercion were in White hands. A Black family could be evicted from its home, the head of household could be fired and/or arrested, welfare assistance could be stopped, or in some instances a family could be burned out or even beaten or killed.

There were 4,742 lynchings in the United States from 1882 to 1968 (three-quarters of them Blacks), of which about 1,500 occurred between

---

[7]   Executive Order 9981: Desegregation of the Armed Forces (1948). "On July 26, 1948, President Harry S. Truman signed this executive order establishing the President's Committee on Equality of Treatment and Opportunity in the Armed Services, committing the government to integrating the segregated military." Accessed June 2, 2014, http://www.ourdocuments.gov/.

1918 and 1968. These hate crimes not only horrified some citizens in the north during those years, but they had the effect of terrorizing whole communities into submission. Not many individuals in any community had the courage to risk death in order to stand up against an entrenched system. Less severe forms of retaliation were much more common and ultimately had the same effect because the news of them spread throughout a small community.[8]

Case in Point: The South Georgia Saga

In September 1868 in Camilla, Georgia, a parade of Negro and White Republicans was attacked by angry White Georgians as it entered the center of town. In the ensuing melee, twelve Negroes were killed, thirty were wounded, and two disappeared altogether. For native White Georgians, Camilla was a successful reassertion of pre-war White power over Blacks.

Are they ready to become the "slaves of slaves"? Herschel V. Johnson described the new constitution as "without parallel in history" and charged that it represented only Blacks. He warned that it would bring "the state of Georgia under the dominion of *Negro supremacy*"; never before had any nation attempted "to elevate the emancipated slave above his recent master, to subordinate the superior to the inferior race, and clothe the latter with the political power of the state.[9]

Despite its "widespread violence against Black and White Republicans" and its "continuation of the Civil War," the Ku Klux Klan was considered a proper and necessary response to the reality of Negro enfranchisement.[10] As a result, the vicious activities of the Klan were supported by the "best people" of the state. The acceptance of racial violence, which had been minimal during the first two years of Reconstruction, escalated wildly as Whites determined to

---

[8]   Dwight D. Murphey. "Lynching: History and Analysis," published in the *Journal of Social and Economic Studies Legal-Studies Monograph Series*, 1995. An abstracted version of the first two parts was published in *Conservative Review*, July/August 1995, 8–15.

[9]   Herschel V. Johnson. *Weekly Courier*, Rome, Georgia, March 27, 1868, 284–5.

[10]   Charles L. Flynn, Jr. (1983). *White Land, Black Labor: Caste and Class in Late Nineteenth Century Georgia*, Baton Rouge, LA: Lousiana State University Press.

neutralize the attraction the Republican Party had for freedmen and poor Whites. Only by driving a wedge between these two elements could the Democrats hope to win the election.

One of the most widely publicized incidents of violence during the brief campaign occurred on the night of March 31, 1868, when several masked men entered the Columbus boarding house where George W. Ashburn lived. Ashburn, a White Republican and a Rufus Bullock supporter, had been a delegate to the constitutional convention. In Columbus, Ashburn had a reputation for cohabiting with Black women, and he seemed to personify the imagined evils Republicanism would lead to. As Ashburn lay sleeping in his bed, masked men fired a number of shots into his body and killed him. His murder served as an object lesson to Georgia's freedmen and their White Republican allies. No refuge was possible, and no armed force was sufficient to withstand the wrath of White Georgians. Despite the best efforts of the Democratic Party, and the Klan, when given the opportunity to vote, freedmen flocked to the polls.

The April victory by the Republicans served only to increase the determination of White Democrats to destroy the political power of the newly enfranchised freedmen. From April until the presidential and congressional elections in November, Democratic pressure in the form of verbal and physical assaults against Black and White Republicans continued. The Klan, now acknowledged by leading Whites to be an essential tool in curtailing Republican influence, spread rapidly throughout the state as the surviving antebellum political leaders gave their approval to the organization. Agents of the Freedmen's Bureau, many of them now full-time federal army officers, noted dramatic increases in the number of violent incidents between Whites and Blacks. In plantation counties in particular, the assaults more than quadrupled in number over those recorded in 1867. During that year, for example, 16 freedmen had been killed and 47 injured. In 1868, following the enfranchisement of Blacks and the success of Republicans in state elections, 75 freedmen were murdered and 203 injured. Of these recorded incidents, 36 murders were listed as the result of Ku Klux Klan activities or were attributed to "political differences." Thirty-three murders were described as having been caused by "unknown" or "other" causes—vague terms that frequently masked political differences. Of the 203 assaults with injuries, 82 were directly attributed to politics, while an additional 101 fell into the category of "unknown" or "other." For these acts of violence, state and federal authorities arrested 37 persons in 1867 but managed to secure only one conviction. In 1868, despite the increase in violence, only 35 arrests were made and only two convictions secured.[11]

Certainly these figures gave dramatic proof to the ominous warning White Georgians were sending to Blacks in Georgia. It was almost a certainty that any act of violence by Whites against Blacks would go unpunished. Throughout the spring and summer of 1868, Democratic papers and party spokesmen warned of impending large-scale riots in the state. The *Milledgeville Federal Union* noted the riot that had occurred in New Orleans in 1867 and predicted that several such riots would sweep Georgia before the presidential election in November. Of course the editor assigned the blame in advance to the Republicans because "their political salvation depends on it, and they have determined to have one come what may."[12] The *Athens Southern Watchman* echoed the *Federal Union* in an editorial that concluded "it is evident from the number and character of the disturbances of the public peace by Negroes in different sections of the state that bad White men are at the bottom of it and hounding these ignorant people on."[13]

Rumors of Blacks arming themselves to meet Klan violence with counterforce persisted. On August 31, the Georgia senate adopted a resolution requesting the governor to issue a proclamation outlawing "violent and unlawful assemblages." On September 2, the lower house concurred with the senate and sent Governor Rufus Bullock a resolution to that effect. On September 4, Bullock made use of his powers as governor to issue a proclamation prohibiting armed assemblies of any kind, exempting only federal troops. Bullock's proclamation lent credence to the rumors circulating that the Union League and the Equal Rights Association, two Republican-financed organizations that provided grass-roots support for the party, had purchased and stored arms for secret Negro militia groups to use on

---

[11]   W. G. Leduc to Dr. James Pinkey Hambleton, September 3, 1868, in the James Pinkey Collection, Emory University Library, Atlanta, Georgia.

[12]   Theodore B. FitzSimons, Jr. "The Camilla Riot," *Georgia Historical Quarterly*, 30 (1951): 116–25.

[13]   Ibid.

Election Day.[14] An armed uprising in Chatham County by freedmen who resisted being dispossessed from abandoned plantations in which they had settled gave additional substance to such rumors.[15] These uprisings became widespread.[16]

In early September, handbills announcing a Republican meeting to be held in Camilla on September 19 were circulated in southwestern Georgia. The purpose of the meeting was to generate support for William P. Pierce, a Republican candidate for Congress, and for John Murphy, a candidate for elector on the Grant ticket. Groups of freedmen from Albany (Georgia) and surrounding areas marched with a fife and drum bandwagon toward Camilla on the designated day. In the town, angry citizens forewarned of the march by a White man named Robert Cochran lined the courthouse square.

As the Republican parade approached the town, it was stopped by Sheriff Mumford S. Poore. Poore asked the group to turn around and abandon their plans for a parade. Noting that some of the freedmen carried rifles and pistols, Poore tried to persuade them to lay aside their weapons. For the Republicans, any backing down in the face of White opposition would be politically disastrous, and they rejected the sheriff's advice. When the marchers continued their march to town, the sheriff left them and hurried into Camilla to organize a posse to deal with the "mob."[17]

As the Republicans entered the town, they were confronted by a drunken White man, James Johns, who ordered the band to stop playing and the freedmen to leave the area. When the marchers refused to obey, Johns fired his shotgun into the crowd. Certain that a trap had

---

[14]   Theodore B. FitzSimons. *"The Camilla Riot,"* 116–25. *Georgia Historical Quarterly*, Vol. 35, No. 2, June 1951.

[15]   W. G. LeDuc to Dr. James Pinkney Hambleton, Sept. 3, 1868. James Pinkney Hambleton Collection, Emory University Library, Atlanta.

[16]   George C. Rabie (1984). *But There Was No Peace: The Role of Violence in the Politics of Reconstruction*. Athens, 109.

[17]   Christian Raushenberg. "Tabular Statement of Assaults and Batteries with Intent to Kill Committed upon Freed People in Division of Albany, State of Georgia, from January 1 to October 31, 1968," roll 32 BRFA L-GA (M798). FitzSimons, using published accounts rather than the original Freedmen's Bureau documents, incorrectly referred to Pierce as N. P. Pierce and to Poore as Munford J. Poore.

been laid for them, the freedmen returned the fire. When the shooting was over, twelve Negroes were killed, thirty were wounded, and two disappeared.[18]

Although Whites in Camilla blamed the entire affair on the Negro marchers, reports filed with Mitchell County Freedmen's Bureau agent Christian Raushenberg told of freedmen hunted down with dogs and horses throughout the night and much of the following day. The Whites in Camilla "did not hesitate but seemed to exalt in following the example of James Johns by firing into the assemblage of the colored people [and] in routing and chasing the unarmed and unresisting fugitives and shooting them down, while running for their lives, and sometimes even after having been wounded, overtaken and after having surrendered themselves to their mercy."[19]

Quickly seized by the Republicans as a campaign issue that would demonstrate how racist and violent the Democrats were, the Camilla affair received extensive coverage in the state Republican press. Nationally, the Camilla riot was used by the Republicans to justify continued enactment and enforcement of more Reconstruction acts. Despite the efforts of the Republicans to use the Camilla incident to the party's advantage, their continued exposure of the riot had a boomerang effect when they failed to report any arrests or convictions of Camilla residents. Instead of working against the Democrats, the Camilla riot confirmed the effectiveness of Democrats in controlling local political affairs and in carrying out, unhampered, a war of vengeance against Black and White Republicans.

As Christian Raushenberg concluded in his report to his superiors in the Freedmen's Bureau, "The colored people from about and south of Camilla dare not come here, and even the few White people who depreciate [sic] this state of affairs are afraid to speak about these things for fear of secret revenge being taken on their person or property."

Republicans who had benefited from the wholesale support of freedmen in the spring elections found this support slipping away in the face of the party's inability to use its resources and those of the state and national governments to protect its members. The failure of the Bullock government to take strong steps against the White

---

[18] Lee W. Formwalt. "The Camilla Massacre of 1868: Racial Violence as Political Propaganda," *Georgia Historical Quarterly* 71 (1987): 399–426.

[19] Ibid.

townspeople of Camilla or even to impose martial law on Mitchell County demonstrated the success of the Democratic campaign of violence and the inherent weakness of the Republican Party in the state.

Coming immediately on the heels of a successful effort by Democrats to expel Negro members of the General Assembly, Camilla confirmed the recovery of the Democratic Party in Georgia. Although Bullock and his supporters continued to occupy the executive branch of state government for a few more months, they controlled nothing else.

In the presidential election in November, the message of Camilla was made even clearer. Horatio Seymour, the Democratic candidate, carried the state. Of Georgia's 132 counties, Grant managed to secure a majority in only 18. Where Bullock had received 83,500 votes in April, Grant could claim only 57,000 barely six months later. In less than a year, the course of Reconstruction had been reversed in Georgia.

The Camilla riot was not an isolated event occurring in an obscure comer of a large state. It was, instead, part of a larger pattern of violence that engulfed the whole of the South from 1867 to 1869. Just like the New Orleans riot of 1866 and the Cross Plains, Alabama reconstruction tragedy, the Camilla riot of 1870 symbolized opposition to Reconstruction, and was a physical expression of the refusal of Southern Whites to recognize the legitimacy of Negro Civil Rights under Republican leadership. The inability of the state and national Republican organizations to deal with these outbreaks of violence validated the claims of White Democrats that they would never tolerate Negro equality. The aim of White violence was to overthrow Reconstruction, and the failure of authorities to arrest and incarcerate the perpetrators of such violence was proof positive that Reconstruction effectively ended less than a year after it had begun. As George C. Rabie has concluded, "The inconsistency of federal reconstruction policy and the strength of southern resistance seem to have doomed the Reconstruction experiment to inevitable collapse. Although Americans have often been loathing conceding that violence may bring about needed change, terrorism in Reconstruction was instrumental in achieving the ends desired by its perpetrators."[20]

---

[20] George C. Rable. "Southern Interests and the Election of 1876: A Reappraisal," *Civil War History*, Vol. 26, No. 4, December 1980, 347–61, 10.1353/cwh.1980.0067, Ohio: Kent State University Press.

The impact of Camilla was clear to White Georgians: violence worked!

Outside large cities, the great majority of Blacks (as many as 90 percent) were employed in unskilled jobs at minimal pay, primarily as domestic workers, manual laborers, farm workers or sharecroppers, cooks and janitors. A small group of teachers, clergy, and a handful of businessmen dominated the top rungs of the Black socioeconomic structure. The Civil Rights Movement of the 1960s forced improvements in many aspects of African American life.

The playing field is still not level, especially for a large underclass, and progress is a rare blessing. Political action on racial equality, once focused on national exposure of the most blatant abuses by die-hard White supremacists, is now more likely to require battle against a faceless, systemic racism protected by the fine print in legislation and corporate policies and procedures. There is preponderance of evidence in support of this assertion. For example, one realizes that for African Americans, the right to vote in America is still legislated, not to mention the years of struggle by citizens of Washington, D.C., to gain statehood, therefore participating in a meaningful way in American governance with a vote. What explanations can be offered for these denials, especially when our democratic principles are prominently espoused abroad even with bloodshed in many instances? "Black folks" have come a long way, but the scale of equality is still tilted, and the pendulum seems to always swing in the wrong direction.

Chapter 2

THE CIVIL RIGHTS MOVEMENT (1954 AND BEYOND)

Injustice anywhere is a threat to justice everywhere.—Martin Luther King, Jr., "Letter from a Birmingham Jail," April 16, 1963.

Efforts to resist oppression of Blacks by Whites in America began long before the 1960s. Individual and small group defiance began soon after the beginning of the slave trade to the New World in the early seventeenth century. These were followed by slave revolts, of which the most famous was the short-lived rebellion in the 1830s led by Nat Turner and a group of fellow slaves. These efforts were typically local, brief, and violently suppressed by the White community. The impact of these rebellions was primarily to alert Whites to be ever more vigilant and harsh in suppressing resistance.

The modern Civil Rights Movement grew into a national force during the 1960s after the Supreme Court and federal agencies made decisions and policy changes that began to chip away at the legitimacy and hegemony of segregation. The Supreme Court decision in *Brown v. Board of Education* in Topeka, Kansas, ruled that "separate but equal" was not an acceptable principle in public schools. Similar cases were brought and won in other locations, but in most cases local officials tried to ignore the decision or resisted implementation.[21]

President Dwight Eisenhower's decision to send federal troops to Little Rock, Arkansas, to enforce school integration helped tip the scale in favor of compliance with court orders. Local officials who complied often found ways to undermine the spirit of desegregation by tolerating harassment of Black students by their White peers and segregating them

---

[21]   *Brown v. Board of Education* (I). The Oyez Project at IIT Chicago-Kent College of Law. Accessed June 2, 2014. http://www.oyez.org/cases/1950-1959/1952/1952_1/.

by classroom within a school. Public facilities were also desegregated by court order but were often closed to avoid implementation. Lawsuits and public pressure also opened up previously all-White workplaces to Black workers, but here again implementation was often subverted by outlandish requirements.

The Voting Rights Act of 1965 placed the power of the federal government behind the principle of "one man, one vote" and placed the burden on local officials to demonstrate that they had in fact removed irrelevant and ridiculous barriers to Black participation in the democratic process.[22]

In a remarkable example of popular civic action, during the eleven years from 1960 to 1971, more than five million Blacks registered to vote in eleven Southern states, increasing the level of registration from 29.1 percent of those eligible to vote to 56.8 percent. The most dramatic change in the voting area came in Mississippi, where denial of the right to vote had been nearly statewide: registration increased from 5.2 percent of those eligible in 1960 to 59.4 percent in 1971.

Many volumes have been written about the impact of the Civil Rights movement and the increase in African American representation on Southern politics. We must continue to examine this impact beyond the late 1950s and the close of the '60s in order to legitimize the work of Dr. Martin Luther King, Jr., and others in Selma, Montgomery, Birmingham, and even Greensboro. In Mississippi, evidence suggests the Civil Rights Movement had not only made it possible for African Americans to win political office during election but to achieve a significant level of employment.[23] In fact, it has been suggested that organized demonstrations and planned mobilizations in Southern states forced the John F. Kennedy administration to suggest legislation aimed at delimiting the level of disparity in the South.[24]

---

[22] Public domain: "Introduction to Federal Voting Rights Laws: The Effect of the Voting Rights Act." US Department of Justice. June 19, 2009. Retrieved from the www, June 2, 2014.

[23] Kenneth Andrews (1977). "The Impact of Social Movements on the Political Process: The Civil Rights Movement and Black Electoral Politics" in American Review Board 800,819.

[24] Ibid. (2001). "Social Movements and Policy Implementation: The Mississippi Civil Rights Movement and the War on Poverty, 1965-1971, *American Sociological Review* 66: 71-95.

But if the argument for the prominence and effectiveness of mass mobilizations on political participation and outcome is to be accepted at face value, the question must then be answered regarding the benefits that accrued as a result of America's positive response to both the march in Selma and the protest for voting rights. Many researchers posit the assumption that political actors respond to shifting political ideologies. In this case, as the population in the South continued to shift in favor of African Americans, there was a sense that African Americans might begin to vote for candidates who took one ideological stance against another. This assertion, coupled with changes in public opinion, made a compelling case in favor of social changes in support of political parity.

In support of this assessment, I borrow from Anthony Chen and his colleagues (2004) of the University of Michigan, Ann Arbor School of Public Policy. In a research funded by the National Science Foundation, the authors utilized Anthony Down's "democratic theory as a frame of reference for explaining ideological commitments and shifts." Darwinism (1957) posits that "policy will reflect policy preferences of the median voter. It is generally assumed that voters are motivated by ideological commitments, parties are interested only in winning elections, and therefore ideology can be one-dimensional." Given these theoretical postulates, it can be assumed that when public opinion shifts, ideological orientations are adjusted and political opinions are realigned. In the case of Southern politics, these realignments occurred in favor of African Americans.[25] At 65 percent, Black voting registration almost paralleled White voting registration in the eleven Southern states for the first time in eighty or so years following Reconstruction.

From the Supreme Court decision in *Brown v. Board of Education* in 1954 to the Mississippi Freedom Summer of 1964 and the 1965 Voting Rights Act, a period of only eleven short years, the struggle for civil rights and an end to legally sanctioned and enforced segregation grew from a local crisis in a distant corner of the national consciousness to become an urgent issue covered daily on the front pages of major newspapers and debated heatedly in Congress.

---

[25] Anthony S. Chen, et al. (2004). "Did the Civil Rights Movement Have an Impact on Public Policy? Evidence for the Passage of State Fair Housing Laws, 1959–65." National Science Foundation Sponsored Research (SES 0000244), University of Michigan, School of Public Policy, Ann Arbor, Michigan.

Many thousands of ordinary citizens participated in protests throughout the South and saw their efforts change the terms of public debate and policy. Many people, young and old, paid a price for their exercise of free speech, from arrests and beatings, to losing jobs and property, to death in a few cases. Students, young adults, and the elderly, all normally powerless, felt the power of popular protest and defiance of the status quo.

The nation's mass media eventually recognized that civil rights protests were a good story. In addition to triumphant campaigns against segregation and discrimination, the 1960s also produced disturbing events. There were four devastating assassinations (John F. Kennedy in 1963, Malcolm X in 1965, Martin Luther King, Jr. in 1968, and Robert Kennedy in 1968). Most of the largest U.S. cities experienced significant battles between citizens and law enforcement, most in response to King's death or incidents of police excesses.

Electoral Politics

Black leaders, empowered by a newly enfranchised population, were able to gain election to public office in rapidly increasing numbers. Several of the largest and many smaller U.S. cities have had Black mayors in the past twenty-five years, including Atlanta, Cleveland, New York, Los Angeles, Chicago, Detroit, Birmingham, New Orleans, and Denver, as well as Washington, D.C.

From 1970 to 1998, the number of Blacks elected to office in education (school boards), law enforcement (sheriffs and district attorneys), city and county offices, and Congress and state legislatures increased from 1,469 to 8,830. The number of Blacks elected to the House of Representatives increased from 17 in 1981 to 40 in 1995.[26]

Beginning as early as 1948, with the "Dixiecrat" presidential candidacy of Strom Thurmond, the White Southern voter became more and more aligned with the Republican Party. This phenomenon

---

[26] Samuel Walker, Cassia Spohn, and Miriam DeLone. "The Color of Justice: Race, Ethnicity, and Crime in America." *Wadsworth Contemporary Issues in Crime and Justice Services*, Fifth Edition. The data on African American elected officials is regularly reported by the Joint Center for Political and Economic Studies, www.jointcenter.org.

appeared first in presidential elections, then in congressional and U.S. Senate contests, and during the last decade or so in state legislatures. So strong is the connection between race and party in the South that in some states, such as Georgia, the congressional delegation is currently made up of a majority of White Republicans with a minority of Black Democrats.

But it has taken fifty years for the Republican Party to show any evidence of inclusion for African Americans at any significant level of the national government. Recently, the Republican Party has attempted to counter the perception that it is unfriendly to Blacks' hopes and needs by recruiting and appointing Blacks to major positions, including the appointment in 2000 of Secretary of State Colin Powell and National Security Advisor Dr. Condoleezza Rice.

Courting "up and coming" African Americans into the leadership of the Republican Party or mainstream American politics may be credited to the successes of the civil rights struggles, especially in the South. But even nationally, the Republican Party continues to target selected African Americans for inclusion. In 1994, J.C. Watts of Eufaula, Oklahoma, was politically supported by the Republican Party and elected to the U.S. Congress, rising to the chairmanship of the House Republican Conference Committee as the fourth-ranking Republican in the U.S. House of Representatives. Although Watts retired from the House after four terms, he continues to enjoy the grace of the party as the chairman of GOPAC, a political action committee that engages in the training of Republican political candidates at the national level.[27]

While Watts represents a growing number of African American Republicans, leader Harold Ford, Jr. of Tennessee represents the Democratic Party in its progressive and courtship role. Ford is a member of several progressive groups, including the new Democratic Coalition, the Congressional Black Caucus, and the Blue Dog Coalition. He became a member of Congress in 1996 at age twenty-six. This new breed

---

[27]   J.C. Watts and Chriss Anne Winston, *What Color is a Conservative? My Life in Politics* (New York: HarperCollins, 2002); Chris Casteel, "Lawmakers Say Goodbye, for Now—Watts Still Uncertain About Future Plan," *Daily Oklahoman*, December 1, 2002; Alton Hornsby, Jr., and Angela M. Hornsby, "Watts, Julius Caesar, Jr. (J.C.)," in "From the Grassroots: Profiles of Contemporary African American Leaders" (Montgomery, Alabama: E-BookTime, LLC, 2006).--See more at: http://www.Blackpast.org/aah/watts-jr-j-c-1957#sthash.hjoquCiF.dpuf.

of African American politicians is crossing party lines and promoting a common agenda. In 2002, Ford joined forces with Republican Representative Tom Osborne of Nebraska to author a bill that would expand opportunities for all Americans to perform some national service. This was a post-terrorist response to the attacks of September 11, 2001. These new, young, and progressive-minded post-civil rights politicians are poised to abrogate the divisions to previously derail several civil rights agenda items.

Apparently, the generational gap may be responsible in part to their untainted outlook. During the 2004 presidential elections, America witnessed the maturity of another post-Civil Rights politician from Illinois when Senator Barack Obama seized the national spotlight at the Democratic National Convention in Boston. At that time, the soon-to-be U.S. senator electrified the audience and brought a fresh look to national issues that would impact minority and African American lives. With his counterpart Jackson, Jr. in the House of Representatives for Illinois, civil rights ideas are expected to blossom and gain national prominence in years to come.

These are just highlights of our believed social contributions of the civil rights movements as we embrace the twenty-first century. These political milestones are complemented by achievements and successes of "sons and daughters" of the Civil Rights Movement such as Representative Eleanor Holmes Norton, Jesse Jackson Sr., Kweisi Mfume, John Lewis, Cynthia McKinney, Carol Moseley Braun (in 1992, Braun became the first African American woman elected to the U.S. Senate), Ambassador Andrew Young, and others who for years have exercised their First Amendment right to free speech in support of civil rights for all Americans while participating in partisan and electoral politics.

While significant strides have been made in the area of electoral politics, current arguments to roll back civil rights successes, especially those involving affirmative action, equal access to education, healthcare and child protection laws, give civil rights organizations such as the NAACP new urgency to retool the machinery of justice and recapture the popular consensus that has served us well so far.

African Americans, like many Americans, continue to uphold the promises of freedom and equality as provided by the U.S. Constitution. The Fourteenth Amendment, as ratified on July 9, 1868, guarantees every born or naturalized citizen of the United States due process and equal protection of the law. This amendment prohibits any exclusionary tactic at the federal or state level aimed at depriving persons from participation in electoral politics, and it prohibits discrimination. Therefore, when African Americans seek redress, they do so with the full understanding that those demands are constitutionally protected.

But in the United States of America, as in many other nation states, power concedes nothing, and rights gained cannot be ignored with the assumption that they are perpetually secured. In our previous discussion, we suggested that when public opinion shifts, political agenda appears to realign. It is during the period of realignment that previous civil rights gains are minimized or reduced if not protected by dynamic political safeguards. For African Americans, history suggests that no time is a good time to take an eye off the prize; to do so would be expensive, to say the least, especially considering the journeys and struggles of the past fifty years.

Who Protects Us While We Sleep?

In the past, we have relied on civil rights organizations such as the NAACP and the SCLC for advocacy. Racial parity was achieved primarily through civil disobedience utilizing nonviolent strategies such as sit-ins, marches, and demonstrations. Martin Luther King, Jr. organized and marched in Birmingham in 1963, thus facilitating the process for dismantling Jim Crow laws and ultimately leading to the legislative enactment of the Civil Rights Act of 1964 and the Voting Rights Act of 1965. In August 1963, the march in Washington aimed at promoting jobs and freedom drew millions to the Washington Mall. These rallies not only mobilized African Americans but White sympathizers as well. The efforts yielded increased political participation for African Americans.

But while its primary protectors were African Americans, the resulting legislation and complementary agendas extended protection and equal rights to other minorities. For African Americans, these strategies were positive and effective. We were protected as we slept because our ideas and arguments were constitutionally relevant and sound but had the tendency to rub negatively on other immigrant groups. The strategy has kept America's crime—slavery—in the forefront and reminds America that it must remedy wrongs of the past regardless of its reluctance if the Constitution is to be upheld.

Today, however, the conscience of the nation is heavy with other issues, especially those relating to a changing political dynamic. African Americans no longer constitute the largest minority group, and public opinion regarding their demands has shifted. "Currently, about one million people a year migrate to the United States, and those who were born on foreign soil now constitute more than 10 percent of the U.S. population—twice the percentage of thirty years ago. Since 1977, four out of five immigrants have come from Latin America or Asia. Hispanics are now overtaking African Americans as the nation's largest minority."[28] Given this demographic reality, it is easy to see why the claim that the nation's goals, focus, and political agenda may change and that past civil right groups may have a difficult task protecting African Americans as they sleep. In order to protect past gains and seek new progress, new frontiers must be emphasized. It is necessary to expand into critical areas thus far seen as protected territories.

I suspect W. E. B. Du Bois was ahead of his time when he suggested, "We seldom study the condition of the Negro today honestly and carefully. It is so much easier to assume that we know it all. Or perhaps having already reached conclusions in our minds, we are loathing having them disturbed by facts. And yet how little do we really know of these millions, of their daily lives and the longings, of their homely joys and sorrows and their real shortcomings. ... All these we can only learn by intricate contact with the masses and not by wholesale arguments."

Based on Du Bois's poetic yet predictive exposé, African American freedom today can only be achieved and sustained by seeking the discovery of new information about the political system. One must juxtapose this new information with old practices in order to derive improved workable solutions devoid of old mistakes. Essentially, in order to obtain political relief, it appears that we cannot wait for the political system to respond to our demands. We can ill-afford this

---

[28]   Steffen W. Schmidt, et al. (2004). *American Government and Politics Today, Brief Edition, 2004-2005*, Belmont, CA: Thomson Wadsworth, 103.

luxury at this historical juncture; we must "agitate"[29] the system and force some action.

Black Southerners are quite familiar with political agitation despite the assumption that many may have been comfortable with their "separate but equal" status. In fact, these authors, Howard Odum and Guy B. Johnson (1944), destroyed these myths when they published their collection of essays by prominent Black intellectuals titled *What the Negro Wants,* which was edited by Howard University historian Rayford Logan. The book called for "equal rights for African Americans and an end to segregation."[30]

So we ask, what does the Negro want in the twenty-first century? And what are the mechanisms for achieving these goals? Suffice it to say African Americans today still want freedom in all its manifestations, a comfortable standard of living, and access to education, healthcare, safety, and security. African Americans are not an exclusive group, nor are they different from other social or ethnic groups in their search for self-worth and social relevance. The instruments and strategies for achieving parity may be different, but the expected outcomes are the same. Some of these growth strategies will be discussed elsewhere in this book.

---

[29] W. E. B. Du Bois (1903). *The Souls of Black Folk, Chapter VIII of the Quest of the Golden Fleece,* Cambridge, MA: University Press.

[30] Agitation as used here means stimulating the system through political action (as used by W. E. B. Du Bois and others at the dawn of the twentieth century).

Chapter 3

EDUCATION THROUGH THE YEARS

The Negro must climb in the achievement of higher things. Race must conquer the Alps of oppression—there should be a will not to surrender. Negro should feel himself a sovereign human being. Man should harness the elements and nature and use them to his will.— Marcus Garvey, *Negro World* editorial headline, October 1, 1921.

Researchers have generally agreed that one of the major strategies for economic and social empowerment and political enfranchisement is education. But in America, education has undergone a transformation in the past fifty years. The overall percentage of students who graduated from high school grew from 47.4 percent in 1945 to 76.4 percent in 1965 but declined to 72.5 percent in 2001. The number of students obtaining bachelor's degrees increased from 136,200 in 1945 (11 percent of high school graduates four years earlier) to 1,282,000 in 2001 (47 percent of high school graduates four years earlier).[31]

The rate at which Blacks graduate from high school has lagged behind Whites, although the gap has narrowed considerably. Since 1967, when the Census Bureau began collecting dropout data by race, the percentage of dropouts among sixteen- to twenty-four-year-olds has dropped for Blacks from 28.6 percent to 10.9 percent, while the rate for Whites in the same age group dropped from 15.4 percent in 1967 to 7.3 percent in 2001.

---

[31] Karen Kruse Thomas. "Dr. Jim Crow: The University of North Carolina, the Regional Medical School for Negroes and the Desegregation of Southern Medical Education 1945–60," *The Journal of African American History*, Vol. 88, No. 3, Summer 2003, 223.

Why Do Students Drop Out?

Blacks gained admittance to law and medical school in increasing numbers during the past twenty-five years. First-year Black law school students increased from 2,128 in 1976–77 to 3,353 in 1999–2000, while total first-year law school enrollment was growing from 39,996 to 43,152. Thus, Blacks represented 5.3 percent of first-year law school enrollees in the 1976–77 academic year, and 7.7 percent in the 1999–2000 academic year, a 45 percent gain.

In 2002, Blacks comprised 7.2 percent of all new medical school students. The number of Black physicians increased by 141 percent (from seventeen thousand to forty-one thousand) between 1983 and 1999, when they comprised 5.7 percent of all physicians in the United States. The proportion of Blacks among all recipients of "first professional degrees," such as law and medical degrees, rose from 4.0 percent in 1976–77 to 6.9 percent in 2000. The number of Blacks conferred first professional degrees grew dramatically from 2,537 in 1976–77 to 5,555 in 1999–2000, an increase of 118 percent. Given the increasing representation of Blacks in professional groups, it is noteworthy that the various Civil Rights legislations have had some impact on equal access to education.[32]

However, while great strides have been made in increasing the representation of Blacks in many professional groups, the increases are miniscule when compared with the total population. One would have expected to see a much larger representation for Blacks fifty years after the striking down of segregation in public accommodation in the *Brown v. Board of Education* case. It is apparent that fifty years after the U.S. Supreme Court's *Brown v. Board of Education* decision, segregation continues to prevail in the American education system. Because of White flight, meaning that large numbers of White families have moved from the inner city to the suburbs, particularly in large metropolitan areas, inner-city school systems are even more disproportionately Black than the general population.

---

[32] US Department of Commerce, Bureau of the Census. "The Social and Economic Status of the Black Population in the United States: A Historical View," 1790–78, 113; data for 1980 obtained from the 1980 Census of Population and Housing; advance report PFi-C80-/-1, p. 4. See also US Center for Educational Statistics and the US Census Bureau.

In communities large and small, segregation in housing often ensures that the school district will have a dominant racial or ethnic population. White parents are much more likely to send their children to private schools than Black parents. Within individual schools, under the guise of ability tracking, students are often segregated, so they end up in classrooms that are much less racially balanced or diverse than the student body as a whole.

National Center for Education Statistics Dropout Prevention Program -- Who is at risk of dropping out?

Several studies have found poor academic performance to be the strongest predictor of risk of dropping out (Hess, et al. 1987; Wood 1994). Other students who are at higher risk of dropping out include those who

- repeat one or more grades
- are from low socioeconomic backgrounds
- speak English as a second language
- become pregnant
- are frequently absent/truant

Why do students drop out?

Schools and districts do not always know why students leave school. Many schools do not require existing students to complete exit surveys or interviews.

When students cite their reasons for dropping out of school, they report various factors. The Oregon Department of Education tracked a cohort of students from 1991-95. At the end of the four-year period, 24.5 percent of the students had dropped out before graduating. The most frequent reason given was "irrelevant coursework." Other reasons were peer pressure, teaching that didn't match student learning styles, and lack of personal attention.

A 1994–95 Texas dropout report provided the top reasons students in Texas decided to leave school. As reported by school districts, these reasons were (in order of frequency):

- poor attendance
- to enter a non-state-approved GED program or employment
- low or failing grades
- age
- to get married
- pregnancy
- suspension/expulsion
- failed exit TAAS/did not meet graduation requirements

With regard to entering non-state approved alternative programs, students of all races from families in the lowest quartile of income were 5.9 times as likely to drop out of high school without graduating (20.7 percent in 2000) than were students from the highest income quartile (3.5 percent). This ratio has hardly changed since 1970, when it was 5.4, based on a dropout rate of 28 percent for the lowest income quartile and 5.2 percent for the highest. This pattern disproportionately affects Black students, who are much more likely to be from low-income families. While this data is specific to Texas, the variables that are used to analyze the reasons for dropout rates appear to be nationally relevant.

Don't Count Me Out – A True Story

Andre, now twenty-two, lives in a small Southern town with a population of seventy-eight thousand. At age twelve, he and his younger brother stole a truck from a neighbor. He was caught joy riding, taken to the youth detention center, and released into the custody of his parents.

After being officially sentenced for the crime, he was placed on probation for twelve months and, as part of his rehabilitation, had to participate in community service and report regularly to his probation officer. He was kicked out of his boyhood home by his mother, and he and his younger brother lived on the street for a while and were eventually placed in foster care as a result of a "good Samaritan" who took them off the street and turned them over to the Department of Family and Children Services. Andre was sent to an alternative school because of disciplinary problems, but by the tenth grade, he straightened up and was given special attention by his teachers. He completed high school and was admitted to a local college. He currently maintains a 3.2 GPA and is on the football team. He works full time and now shares an apartment with his younger brother, who also attends a local college.

Andre was labeled a problem youth once he committed a crime, and such social stigmas are often not acceptable in mainstream schools. Students with such social labels are often not expected to perform, remain in school, and/or succeed. Andre's story reveals the prescriptive nature of teachers' perceptions. Andre could have been counted out in the tenth grade.

This story adds to the dilemma that accompanies the relationship between teacher and student-affecting perception, behavior, learning, and success, especially if a student happens to be African American. It is the systemic view of Andre's situation that may also contribute to the high rate of school dropouts today.

Andre's story demonstrates the dilemma of teacher perception and ability tracking. The prevailing assumption that children from disadvantaged backgrounds cannot learn or that poverty predetermines children's future places severe limitations on student learning and outcome. Ability tracking is a major factor in school segregation because it utilizes socioeconomic constructs as determinants for success; nothing could be further from the truth. But despite its analytical and pedagogical flaws, ability tracking has been used routinely for decades and justified as a means of gearing instruction to the needs and capabilities of students. While a case can be made for ability tracking, it has often had the effect (deliberate or not) of segregating students, putting minority students on a vocational track, and White students on a college preparatory track. Sometimes the segregation is at the school system level as a result of White flight to suburban communities, where school boards can gear their policies to the children of affluent families, providing a college preparatory curriculum, advanced placement courses, and proactive college counseling. Sometimes segregation visible at the school level is fostered by housing segregation based on race and income, so that some schools are predominantly Black and others are predominantly White. Here again, resources can be geared toward college or vocational objectives, reinforced by teacher attitudes, discipline and security policies, hiring patterns, and course availability.

Teacher Attitude and Student Performance

In a society such as ours where color and ethnicity apparently define one's character, it is not uncommon to see race as being a pathological determinant for success in school. In White America, White teachers hold ideological biases regarding African American culture, and this sometimes controls and shapes teacher attitude toward the student, especially if the teacher happens to be White and the student African American.

In support of this assertion, Christine Sleeter published an article on school bias, in which she contends, "For a White teacher to challenge his or her own complicity with the racist institutions, customs, and ideologies that persist to dominate, dis-empower, and exploit people of color, means for that teacher to challenge his or her own identity. Thus, White educators who genuinely seek to empower and help their students face this moral dilemma of choosing between the sanctity of their own identities (including the privileges of that identity) and identifying with their students, which means challenging their own identity."[33]

Judith Blau and her colleagues believe America is still struggling with the idea of accommodating cultural diversity even fifty years after *Brown v. Board of Education* because "it emphasizes rights for individuals as detached persons and not as one of their rights to identify group membership and social roots."[34]

But on balance, White teachers are not the only ones who hold narrow perspectives about African American culture; hence non-White teachers, even African American teachers, misread Black youths' attitudes in schools and often link them to a potential for failure. Not only do teachers' attitudes toward culturally differentiated attitudes by Black youth affect teacher/student relations, teachers' expectations also affect student learning outcome. Children's personalities, learning styles, and home environment may contribute to students' reactions to a learning environment. It may make them appear alert and bright at one time, and inattentive and slow at other times. An African American child, or any child for that matter, who arrives at school sleepy, hungry, worried, or sloppily dressed can seem to be resistant to authority or to learning, or considered uncooperative or slow. Since many teachers bring their own prejudices and preferences to the classroom, this misdirected, misinformed, and culturally insensitive bias creates a myopic view that is antithetical to teachers' expectations. African American school-age children have suffered these miscues for decades; it is not surprising then that many have been labeled and assumed to be suffering from attention deficit disorder (ADD) or hyperactivity. In many cases, teachers have refused to teach them. Many children have been placed in special education programs that fail to rehabilitate but reinforce the perceived training and learning disability.

A particular case comes to mind. Little Johnny (not his real name) attends a rural school in the Midwest. He was said by his previous teachers to be untalented and destined for failure. Johnny seldom turns in his homework, so his academic talents are hidden from his teachers. His parents have not attended scheduled conferences by the teachers,

33   Christine E. Sleeter (1996). *Multicultural Education as Social Activism,* New York: SUNY Press, 65.

34   Judith Blau, et al. (2004). *Race in Schools: Perpetuating White Dominance,* Boulder, CO: Lynn Rienner Publishers.

and these situations also negatively influence teachers' views of Johnny's future. The apparent lack of concern by Johnny and his parents is also indicative of a lack of student motivation and parental involvement or willingness, especially since Johnny seems uninterested in class and even hostile at times.

But is this type of behavior by Johnny suggestive of who Johnny really is, especially since there are countless instances and documented evidence that link poor performance to other variables outside the schoolyard? For example, one would expect a good teacher to enquire whether Johnny has a problem at home that commands his attention, because it appears that accepting Johnny's behavior now as a prescription for failure may be shortchanging his potential for success.

Of course Johnny's case is not isolated; there are numerous documented instances across America where "Johnny" appears over and over again, and similar assessments are offered. Reactions appear to be similar and consistent. Recall the Pygmalion Effect,[35] where teachers assumed they were dealing with superior students when, in fact, that was not the case since students in the group were randomly selected. In fact, at the end of the experiment, students in grades one and two particularly exhibited superior performance in IQ tests over other students with similar ability. The results were so revealing and caused the researchers to issue a clear indictment about teacher expectations.

Researchers noted that teacher expectation and behavior influenced students' performance and intellectual growth. The lesson here is that because the teachers perceived the group of students as special and highly intellectual, their behavior toward the students was also positive. Rosenthal and Jacobson's Pygmalion study has generated tremendous controversies, and its findings have been replicated many times, causing some researchers to conclude that perhaps "Johnny can't read" because

---

[35] In 1914, George Bernard Shaw wrote *Pygmalion,* a comedy that featured character Eliza Doolittle. It was suggested that a person's place in society is largely conditioned by how others view and/or treat him or her. Robert Rosenthal and Leonine Jacobson used the play as a frame of reference where teachers were given false information about the learning abilities of selected students in their 1968 publication *Pygmalion in the Classroom* to conclude that students' intellectual development is a response to teachers' expectations. See http://www.duq.edu/about/centers-and-institutes/center-for-teaching-excellence/teaching-and-learning/pygmalion.

his teachers lack faith in his reading ability—especially if he is poor and/ or belongs to a minority group. Whether one accepts this "expectancy theory" or not, it is still dominant today, and perhaps it will continue to have psychoanalytical relevance in student learning.

The above may offer partial explanation as to why Black students are twice as likely to drop out of school, are less likely to take academically challenging courses, and are less likely to go to college if they do graduate. Perhaps the problem is partially economic, in that students from families in the lowest income quartile (whatever their race) are several times more likely to drop out of school than are students from families in the highest income quartile.

Let us look at the numbers. A result from the 2008–11 American community survey published by the United States Census Bureau shows that in 2011, there is an increase of roughly two million Black college students from eighteen years earlier. About 80 percent of African Americans age twenty-five and older have a high school diploma, and the percentage of persons with baccalaureate degrees increases by two percentage points to 19 percent. These numbers are still about ten points below the national average.

The U.S. Department of Education, the Institute of Education Sciences, and the National Center for Educational Statistics compared the educational achievement of all minority groups in the United States and found that "overall, Hispanic adults in the United States had lower rates of high school attainment than adults of other racial/ethnic groups. In 2008, about 62 percent of Hispanic adults over the age of twenty-five had completed at least a high school equivalency, while 92 percent of Whites, 89 percent of Asian/Pacific Islanders, 83 percent of Blacks, and 78 percent of American Indian/Alaskan Natives had done so."

Furthermore, in 2008, "[t]hirteen percent of Hispanic adults and 15 percent of American Indian/Alaskan Native adults had obtained at least a bachelor's degree, and 52 percent of Asian/Pacific Islanders, 33 percent of Whites and 20 percent of Black had done so."[36] While the rising rates in educational achievement mark a significant shift and increase over the past twenty years, the question one ponders is why do Blacks continue to lag behind?

Debates about the causes of failure in school alternate between blaming the parents, blaming social conditions (too much television, drugs, sex, immorality), or blaming the students (they are lazy, unappreciative, have an attitude). Some have even suggested that school administrations and faculty members contribute to racial disparities as well.

Parenting styles can encourage children to ask questions and explore new experiences or, conversely, to be withdrawn. By any standard, a society is better served by increasing the number of high school and college graduates than by increasing the number of prison inmates. The former add to the public wealth, while the latter are a burden on the public wealth. It has been documented that the United States has the highest incarceration rate in the world. In fact, since 2002, prison populations have increased in some parts of the world; the natural rate of incarceration for countries comparable to the United States tends to stay around one hundred prisoners per one hundred thousand population.

"The US rate is 500 prisoners per 100,000 residents, or about 1.6 million prisoners in 2010, according to the latest available data from the Bureau of Justice Statistics."[37] Among the forty states surveyed, representing more than 1.2 million inmates (of 1.4 million total people incarcerated in all fifty state prison systems), the total per-inmate cost

---

[36] The data is drawn from the U.S. Department of Education's National Center for Educational Statistics article titled "Status and Trends in the Education of Racial and Ethnic Groups." In examining the educational progress and challenges facing minorities in the United States in the area of education, the report documents that over time (analysis presented from 2007 to 2008), there is a slight increase in the number of students in each of the minority and ethnic groups who have completed high school and progressed to college. However, the increase is still below the national average.

[37] Paul Guerino, Paige M. Harrison, and William J. Sabol. "Prisoners in 2010" (Revised), Washington, D.C.: Bureau of Justice Statistics, 2011; and Sara Wakefield and Christopher Uggen, "Incarceration and Stratification," *Annual Review of Sociology* 36 (2010): 387–406.

averaged \$31,286 and ranged from \$14,603 in Kentucky to \$60,076 in New York.[38]

Educational Attainment

Young African Americans between twenty-five and twenty-nine years old are more likely to have high school diplomas and college degrees than older African Americans. Thus, disparity in educational attainment is more pronounced when viewed from the perspective of the whole adult population over age twenty-five. This disparity, of course, reflects social conditions that prevailed as many as four decades ago, when those who are sixty today were in school, as well as the more recent environment. In 1970, more than twice as high a proportion of White adults had finished a bachelor's degree (11.8 percent) than had Black adults (4.5 percent), a gap of 7.3 percentage points. In 1999, the White rate had risen to 27.8 percent, while the Black rate grew to 15.4 percent, a gap of 12.4 percentage points.[39]

---

[38] "The average per-inmate cost (\$31,286) was calculated by dividing the total taxpayer cost of prisons in forty states (\$38,903,304,484) by the total number of inmates in these states (1,243,487). The average per-inmate cost in these forty states—i.e., the average of the forty per-inmate costs tabulated in figure 4—is \$31,979. The total number of inmates in fifty state prisons (1.4 million) was obtained from the Pew Center on the states' report "Prison Count 2010," p. 1. This information is obtained from the Vera Institute of Justice's Center on Sentencing and Corrections titled "Price of Prisons: What Incarceration Costs Taxpayers," January 2012. http://jjie.org/vera-institute-report-american-taxpayers-spent-nearly-billion-last-year-on-incarceration-expenses/.

[39] "In this indicator, educational attainment represents the achievement of at least the cited credential (i.e., a high school diploma or equivalency certificate, a bachelor's degree, or a master's degree). Between 1990 and 2012, educational attainment among twenty-five- to twenty-nine-year-olds increased: the percentage who had received at least a high school diploma or its equivalent increased from 86 to 90 percent, and the percentage who had completed a bachelor's degree or higher increased from 23 to 33 percent. In 2012, some 7 percent twenty-five- to twenty-nine-year-olds had completed a master's degree or higher, a 3 percentage point increase from 1995 according to the national center for educational statistics." This information is obtained from the National Center for Educational Statistics, 1999.

Educational attainment is generational. Based on the aforementioned study by the National Center for Educational Statistics, the overall Black high school dropout rate for sixteen- to twenty-four-year-olds is 13.7 percent among Blacks (nearly double the White rate, 7.7 percent), whereas the rate among Black teens from low-income families is 24 percent, compared with 9.6 percent from middle-income and 0.8 percent from high-income families. In fact, the dropout rate among high income Blacks is half as much as the rate for high income Whites (1.9 percent). It should be noted that the dropout rate for Hispanics is more than double that of the Black rate (29.4 percent) and very high (44.7 percent) for Hispanic students from low-income families. Comparing the current data with the previous discussion helps in highlighting the slow progress that has been made in closing the minority education achievement gap. (See Table 1 for a complete breakdown of the level of educational attainment among minority and ethnic groups.)

Over the years, attempts were made to narrow this gap, but in many instances, such attempts were too little and too late because many minorities twenty-five and older had already fallen through the cracks or lost hope of meeting up in the race or of winning the race for equality at all.

Table 1

Standard errors for percentage distribution of adults twenty-five and older according to highest level of educational attainment, by race/ethnicity: Selected years: 1996–2008.

Race/ Ethnicity and Year	Less than high school completed	At least high school completion				At least a bachelor's degree			
		Total	High school completion	Some college	Associate degree	Total	Bachelor's degree	Master's degree	Doctorate or first professional degree
1996	0.16	0.16	0.19	0.15	0.10	0.17	0.15	0.09	0.06
2000	0.13	0.13	0.17	0.14	0.10	0.16	0.14	0.09	0.06
2004	0.09	0.09	0.12	0.10	0.07	0.11	0.10	0.06	0.04
2008	0.08	0.08	0.11	0.09	0.07	0.11	0.10	0.07	0.04
White									
1996	0.16	0.16	0.22	0.18	0.12	0.20	0.17	0.11	0.07
2000	0.14	0.14	0.20	0.16	0.12	0.19	0.17	0.11	0.07
2004	0.09	0.09	0.14	0.11	0.09	0.14	0.12	0.08	0.05

2008	0.08	0.08	0.14	0.11	0.09	0.14	0.12	0.08	0.05
Black									
1996	0.62	0.62	0.68	0.56	0.36	0.49	0.43	0.24	0.13
2000	0.48	0.48	0.56	0.47	0.30	0.44	0.37	0.24	0.11
2004	0.32	0.32	0.39	0.32	0.22	0.31	0.27	0.16	0.09
2008	0.30	0.30	0.38	0.32	0.23	0.32	0.27	0.17	0.09
Hispanic									
1996	0.80	0.80	0.70	0.54	0.34	0.47	0.40	0.21	0.15
2000	0.51	0.51	0.46	0.35	0.22	0.32	0.27	0.15	0.11
2004	0.32	0.32	0.29	0.22	0.15	0.21	0.18	0.10	0.07
2008	0.29	0.29	0.28	0.21	0.14	0.21	0.18	0.10	0.06
Asian/Pacific Islander									
1996	0.73	0.73	0.81	0.64	0.51	0.97	0.88	0.57	0.44
2000	0.64	0.64	0.75	0.60	0.46	0.90	0.82	0.53	0.43
2004	0.43	0.43	0.52	0.39	0.33	0.64	0.59	0.42	0.33
2008	0.34	0.34	0.43	0.33	0.27	0.54	0.50	0.38	0.27
American Indian/ Alaska Native									
1996	2.01	2.01	2.12	1.81	1.16	1.41	1.06	0.85	0.56
2000	1.76	1.76	1.94	1.65	1.18	1.41	1.22	0.69	0.40
2004	1.61	1.61	1.79	1.59	1.21	1.36	1.12	0.72	0.48
2008	1.28	1.28	1.47	1.28	0.87	1.11	0.93	0.58	0.37

SOURCE: U.S. Department of Commerce, Census Bureau, Current Population Survey (CPS), Annual Demographic Supplement, 1996, 2000, 2004, and Annual Social and Economic Supplement, 2008. This table is adopted from the National Center for Educational Statistics/Institute of Education Sciences. The article is titled "Status and Trends in the Education of Racial and Ethnic Minorities."

There is no surprise then that in 1997, Congress authorized the federal Hope Scholarship program, inspired by a Georgia program of the same name, begun in 1993. A study of the Georgia program by Bridget Terry Long concluded that while this program stimulated an increase in the percentage of eighteen- to nineteen-year-old students attending college by 7 to 8 percent, the effect was primarily among middle-class White students in Georgia. According to Long, however, the program "widened the gap in college attendance between Blacks and Whites and between those from low- and high-income families."[40] Georgia's scholarship program, which provides financial aid only for students attending Georgia institutions, also tended to draw Black students away from predominantly Black institutions in nearby states and motivate them to attend Georgia institutions.

The federal government and the states have recently ushered in a new generation of student-aid policies. These new programs differ from traditional need-based student aid in one crucial way: they are aimed not at low-income students but middle-class students. For example, the federal Hope Scholarship and the Lifetime Learning Credit, provided by 26 USC § 25A(b), is available to taxpayers who have incurred education expenses. For this credit to be claimed by a taxpayer, the student must attend school on at least a part-time basis. The credit can be claimed for education expenses incurred by the taxpayer, the taxpayer's spouse, or the taxpayer's dependent.

This credit allows for a 20 percent tax credit for first $10,000 of qualified tuition and expenses to be fully creditable against the taxpayer's total tax liability. The maximum amount of the credit is $2,000 per household.[41] Similarly, the tax-advantaged college savings plans recently introduced by the federal government and by forty-one states is most attractive to high-income families who have the highest marginal tax rates and saving rates.

How will this new type of student aid affect college attendance rates? Will aid to middle- and high-income families actually increase college attendance, or are the new programs simply transfers to students who would have gone to college anyway? In "Hope for Whom? Financial Aid for the Middle Class and Its Impact on College Attendance," (NBER Working Paper No. 7756), Susan Dynarski estimates the impact of subsidies on the college attendance of middle- and upper-income youth by evaluating Georgia's HOPE (Helping Outstanding Pupils Educationally) Scholarship, the inspiration for the federal Hope Scholarship.

---

[40] Bridget Terry Long (2003). "How do Financial Aid Policies affect Colleges? The Institutional Impact of the Georgia HOPE Scholarship," *The Journal of Human Resources*, Vol. 39, No. 4, Autumn 2004.

[41] http://www.irs.gov/publications/p970/ar02.html#en_US_2011_ publink1000255787. This is an IRS publication that details the complete policy specification for tax and related educational credits.

In 1993, Georgia initiated the HOPE Scholarship, which is funded by state lottery. The program pays for tuition and fees at Georgia's public colleges for state residents who maintain at least a B average in high school and college. Using data from the current population survey, and a set of nearby states as a control group, Dynarski finds that among those youths most likely eligible for Georgia HOPE scholarships, the attendance rate has risen by nearly 11 percentage points relative to attendance of a similar population in nearby states.[42]

This increase is concentrated among Georgia's White students, who have experienced a 12.3 percentage point rise in their enrollment rate relative to Whites in nearby states. The Black enrollment rate, however, appears unaffected by HOPE. The differential impact of HOPE on Blacks and Whites is likely attributable to the focus of HOPE on middle- and upper-income students who perform well in high school. In particular, during the period under study, HOPE provided almost no benefits to the lowest-income students, since the scholarship was reduced dollar for dollar by other sources of aid, including the need-based Pell Grant.

Dynarsky concludes that the results of the Georgia analysis should be applied cautiously to other programs, such as the federal Hope Scholarship. Key institutional differences between the Georgia and federal subsidies suggest that the impact of the federal Hope Scholarship may be less than what Georgia experienced with its program.[43]

Low expectations are now institutionalized as school administrators explain their students' poor performance by citing "adverse demographics," such as the proportion of Black and poor students. School administrators can in fact go to databases at state and national levels, enter their demographic profiles, and retrieve data on the performance of other school systems with similar demographics. In other words, the poor performance of a predominantly Black school system or school can be blamed on the students and their background, excusing those responsible for their education from

---

[42]   Susan Dynarski (2000). "Hope for Whom? Financial Aid for the Middle Class and Its Impact on College Attendance," NBER Working Papers #7756, National Bureau of Economic Research, Inc.

[43]   Ibid.

taking responsibility for helping them achieve at the same levels as their White counterparts.

Of course parents cannot be excluded from the analysis about what is wrong with the system. They have a significant role to play in the preparation of their youth for learning outside the home. But the prevailing notion is that a hungry child cannot learn. This points to poverty as a core issue. But regardless of how learning is viewed, presented, or received by children, socioeconomic determinants seem to drive a wedge between teachers, schools, and parents. The loser seems to be the child.

Lessons from an Innovation

A kindergarten teacher in a rural South Georgia town has, on her own initiative, developed a curriculum with which she is able to teach an entire classroom of average five-year-olds to read at fourth- and fifth-grade levels. She constantly promotes the idea in class that each child can achieve beyond his or her own expectations, regardless of family background or personality. Through the use of cartoon characters presented as role models, she is able to engage children so effectively that they become avid readers, surprising their parents as they read newspaper articles and books thought to be far beyond them. They develop a love of reading so strong that they will tackle any written material.

This method, called young unlimited minds institute (YUMI), engages children and utilizes their love of games and problem solving to inspire learning in an environment of cooperation and positive reinforcement.

Unfortunately, despite a national campaign to improve reading skills at the elementary school level, the teacher who developed the YUMI method has been criticized by some of her colleagues at school and by district administrators for not "following the program" prescribed for kindergarteners. Notable is the school librarian's comment that the teacher's students should not be allowed to check out books because "kindergarteners are not supposed to be reading." The standards adopted by the Georgia Department of Education state kindergarteners are expected to be able to recognize their name and do a few other rudimentary readiness skills by the end of the school year. How meaningful are these criteria in light of the YUMI program?

Chapter 4

POSTINDUSTRIALIZATION AND POPULATION SHIFTS

Rural development, in my view, is the venture capitalist for rural America. It is with this vision in mind that we carry out our mission to first, increase economic opportunity, and second, improve the quality of life for all rural residents through programs that are administered by the Rural Housing Service, the Rural Business Cooperative Service, and the Rural Utility Service.—Thomas C. Dorr, U.S. undersecretary for rural development at the hearing on housing in America of the House Subcommittee on Housing and Community Opportunity, and the Committee on Financial Services, Washington, D.C., July 8, 2003.

Mechanization of farms, particularly in the South, prompted millions of Blacks to migrate to the northeast, Midwest, and west from before the First World War into the 1960s. This exodus affected the foundation of life of African Americans as revenues and other forms of sustenance from sharecropping began to dwindle. This trend came to a standstill in the 1970s and '80s and began to reverse itself in the '90s.

In 1920, Black farmers numbered more than nine hundred thousand, but as they lost or sold their land, their numbers dwindled to a mere eighteen thousand, according to the Agricultural Census of 1997. The losses suffered by African American farmers were similar to those of small farmers across the nation, but their racial disposition, exacerbated by extreme poverty and outright discriminatory laws, helped seal their fate.

At least partially in response to the increasing proportion of Blacks in large cities, White families had also been migrating to suburbs, where effective property tax rates were lower and the burden of city services was lighter. This movement left some central city governments and school systems with a depleted tax base just as demand for city services was increasing. Many of the suburbanites became users of city streets, public facilities, transit systems, police and fire departments, and solid waste systems without directly contributing to the revenue base that supported this infrastructure. For African Americans, the loss of farms and family as a central means of livelihood ensured a poverty-driven life.

According to a Brookings Institution study, "The number of Whites living in high-poverty neighborhoods—where the poverty rate is 40 percent or higher—declined by a dramatic 24 percent, or 2.5 million people, in the 1990s," while those of African American descent continued to rise. While not conclusive, there are reasons that suggest why the socioeconomic conditions of Blacks are a compelling departure from those of Whites. Significant among these reasons is the issue of population movements.

One of the most significant trends of the twentieth century was the massive migration of Black families and individuals from Southern plantations and sharecropping on small farms to large cities in the north. This migration was the product of farm mechanization (which greatly reduced the need for unskilled farm labor), concentration of ownership in large capital-intensive operations, and the growth of national markets for agricultural commodities, including most of the largest crops in American agriculture.

Between 1940 and 1970, an average of 23.3 percent of Black males age twenty to twenty-four migrated out of the Southern states, while only 4.5 percent of Whites in the same age group did so. This trend slowed during the 1970s to 2.1 percent of Black males aged twenty to twenty-four, while White males in the same age group actually experienced a net gain migration. During the 1940s alone, 9.5 percent of the total Black population migrated between non-contiguous states (typically from one region to another), while only 5 percent of Whites did so. (Figures are based on decennial census of population for years mentioned and they are derived from the United States Census Bureau.)

Migration out of the South exacerbated land loss in that when a landowner died, some or all of his or her heirs, now settled in a northern city and perhaps uninterested in using the land, often would sell the inheritance to a buyer equipped to take advantage of the opportunity.

During the 1990s, census data clearly points to a reversal of the seventy-year-old trend toward migration from the South. Presumably, this new trend is the result of several factors:

(1) the economic and population boom in large Southern cities, especially Atlanta, the leading destination of Blacks migrating from North to South,

(2) the gradual disappearance of open forms of discrimination, and

(3) a greater degree of mobility conferred by education, and the ability to compete for good jobs.

But while migration alone cannot be held accountable for negative economic performance by Blacks, it contributed to the loss of whatever wealth Blacks had in terms of real estate. This dwindling wealth is usually exacerbated by a declining viability of the family farm. The family farm supported a commodity market that was locally anchored for the most part. This loss spurred competition for foods across state lines, creating an impossible competition, especially for small farmers.

In 2012, the U.S. Census Bureau released its report that shows a changing American population. Population shifts and related discussions took a backseat while America became and continues to debate issues of demographic change. The census report shows that "White births" now constitute the minority in the United States. From July 2011 to 2012, "Asians, Blacks, Hispanics, and mixed races made up 50.4 percent of all births, becoming a majority for the first time in the history of the United States."

Jennie Wood of *Infoplease* contends:

… the United States had been headed toward a shift in the majority for years. The country was founded by European Whites who depended heavily on enslaved African populations. The 1960s Civil Rights movement and acceptance of interracial marriages sped up the shift. The census data also suggested that the increasing number of Latin Americans immigrating to the United States accelerated the decline of the White birth majority. From 2000 to 2010, more Hispanic births were recorded in the U.S. than Hispanics moving into the country. With the Hispanic population at the median age of twenty-seven in 2012, the trend was expected to continue increasing. The largest single share of total births still belonged to Whites with 49.6 percent. The 2010 census data showed that Whites also remained the majority in the overall U.S. population at 63.4 percent. However, with shift in majority births, the U.S. passed a demographic milestone, moving away from a White baby boomer culture toward a more global, multiethnic country.[44]

Declining Viability of the Family Farm—"Forty Acres and a Mule"

Judge Paul L. Friedman began his 1999 decision in *Pigford v. Glickman,* the successful class-action suit brought by African American farmers, with that familiar broken promise from the Civil War/Reconstruction era. The case concerned the sorry Civil Rights record of the US Department of Agriculture (USDA) and its denial of federal benefits to Black farmers in the years after World War II and in particular the thirty-five years since the Civil Rights Act of 1964. The decline of Black farmers alter World War II contrasted dismally with their gains in the half century after emancipation when, demonstrating tremendous energy and sagacity, they negotiated a maze of racist law and custom and— during the harshest years of segregation, peonage, and violence—gained land and standing in southern communities. By 1910, African Americans held title to some sixteen million acres of farmland; by 1920, there were 925,000 Black farms in the country. In the teens and twenties, however, the graph of rising ownership faltered and then plunged downward. Depression, mechanization, and discriminatory federal programs devoured Black farmers, but their fate was eclipsed by press coverage of school segregation, voting rights,

---

[44] To read a detailed analysis of trends in U.S. population, read *The Population Shifts in the United States* @ Infoplease.com, published by Jennie Wood in 2007 and the discussion regarding a dwindling "White birth." Infoplease is a publication of Pearson Education, Inc. http://www.infoplease.com/us/statistics/population-majority-no-more.html#ixzz32ZDh6Fjk.

and public accommodations. They almost disappeared without a trace.[45]

It is a well-documented fact that in the Southern United States, African Americans constituted large farming populations during the Jim Crow era and continued to do so even after the civil rights struggles of the 1960s.[46] The fundamental issue about American population shifts and changes in demographics begs the question as to what the impact of these changes would have on American agricultural enterprise. Commodity markets are a product of the fact that agricultural products can be bought and sold and transported across the country. The cost of production continues to rise, making it difficult for many Blacks to continue to farm even while their landholdings remain steady. Black farmers cannot compete in a market that was unequally structured in the beginning, and they are fast becoming a dying breed. In effect, corn raised in Nebraska must compete with corn raised in North Dakota or Georgia, regardless of the costs of producing the crop. A bumper crop in one region can lower the prices everywhere else, even where weather or disease destroys most of the crop. For many farmers, the cost of production is often higher than the value of the crop.

In fact, it is this concern for Black farmers that compelled the Congressional Black Caucus (CBC) to hold a rally in March 1999 where Congresswoman Eva M. Brown, an African American Democrat from North Carolina, uttered the following words to encourage Black farmers: "There is reason to despair. ... There are several reasons why the number of Black farmers is declining so rapidly. But the one that has been documented time and time again is the discriminatory environment present in the Department of Agriculture ... the very agency established to accommodate the special needs of farmers. ...

[45] *Pigford v. Glickman*, 185 FRD 82 (DDC 1999), at 85. On property owning, see Loren Schweninger: *Black Property Owners in the South, 1790-1915* (Urbana 1990), 143–237; and Loren Schweninger, "A Vanishing Breed: Black Farm Owners in the South, 1651–1982," *Agricultural History*, Vol. 63, Summer 1989, 41–60.

[46] See Banks, Vera J. and Judith Z. Kalbacher, "The changing U.S. farm population." *Rural Development Perspective*, March 1980, 43-46. Also read: Spencer Wood and Jess Gilbert, "Returning African American farmers to the land: Recent trends and policy rationale," *The Review of Black Political Economy*, Spring 2000.

Once land is lost, it is very difficult to recover. ... We stand here today in despair over this history. Yet we also stand here today in hope that justice will prevail, and that the record will be set right for those farmers who have been wronged. ..."[47]

On the whole, American farming is capital intensive, which means a farm owner must be able to purchase and pay for equipment in good years and bad. This high fixed cost makes the farm owner more vulnerable to crop losses and low prices. A labor-intensive operation, on the other hand, can shift part of the burden of crop losses and low prices to the labor force in the form of reduced employment.

Agricultural economists generally agree that over the past fifty years, the farmer's share of the consumer's food dollar has dropped significantly. Nationwide distribution systems add transport and storage costs, processors add costs, middlemen (shippers, wholesalers, suppliers, and retailers) add layers of profit, and large corporate retailers seek to increase their profits. Small farmers have limited ability to access the food market at a profitable level.

"In fact, the farmer's share of the retail food dollar has been on the decline for more than sixty years. In 1950, farmers received more than forty cents for every food dollar that consumers spent in the grocery store. Today, they receive a paltry nineteen cents."[48]

Attempts to Reverse the Decline of African American Farm Ownership

The Federation of Southern Cooperatives, founded in 1969, was born out of the Southern Civil Rights Movement. Motivated by the rapid decline of Black farm ownership, a small cadre of former civil rights workers and community activists began to organize farmer cooperatives and credit unions and provide technical assistance to Black farmers in improving their production methods and management skills in order

---

[47] Remarks of Congresswoman Eva M. Clayton, The Black Farmers' Demonstration, Washington, D.C., March 2, 1999.

[48] For a complete discussion on the dwindling profit for Black farmers, hence to decreasing interest in farming, see "The Hands that Feed," a project of the FarmPolicyFacts.org., Arlington, VA. Retrieved May 23, 2014, www.thehandthatfeedsus.org.

to make these small farms more viable. Technical assistance can help, but it does not change financial and economic realities.

In 1990, the Federation and other allied groups filed their first lawsuit, followed by a 1997 suit against the USDA alleging that pervasive racism within its corps of county agents and financial agencies placed an onerous and unequal burden on Black farmers over a period of decades and in fact caused many to fail and many others to reap meager results from their labors. The lawsuit resulted in protracted legal and procedural struggles, but it finally culminated in a settlement in 1999 in favor of the Black farmers. Since then, settlements have gone to many Black farmers with an aggregate value of nearly a billion dollars.[49]

While the suit was a historic victory that established the reality and impact of governmentbacked racism, the settlement in most cases did not really change the long-term potential of Black-owned farms. By the time the case was settled, many of the beneficiaries of the court victory were retired or planning for retirement.

With continued difficulties in access to capital, there are limited opportunities to pursue alternative markets, crops and methods of production, including value-added enterprises that can significantly alter the conditions of production. Both Black and White small farmers continue to lose ground (literally and figuratively) in competition with larger corporate farms.

The economic influence of racism can be seen in Southern African American farm laborers, who labored for depressed wages in an unfree market. Classical economic theory, which posits that wage rates in one setting are based on the opportunities available to people of similar skills in other settings, would somehow need to take into account racial segregation in the job market in order to explain how a group of workers could find it necessary to work for minimal wages under punishing conditions. In a social system permeated by unofficial racial discrimination, an apparent economic opportunity may be closed to applicants of the "wrong" color.

---

[49] *Pigford v. Dan Glickman*, US District Court for the District of Columbia, Civil Action No. 97-1978 (PLF). Paul L. Friedman, US District Judge. "The Pigford Case: USDA Settlement of a Discrimination Suit by Black Farmers," Tadlock Cowan, Congressional Research Service, January 13, 2009. Retrieved May 27, 2014.

Societies develop infrastructures to accommodate their population, but corresponding areas where high poverty exists do not usually attract development, so planners and often face negative results when attempting to upgrade poverty-driven areas. Based on this assessment, it is not completely naive to suggest that broken Black families without any significant means of subsistence who were driven out of their farms by mechanization and forced migration would become a less-than-attractive economic entity. Whether these migrations are intentional or not, one thing is clear: urban community and economic development planners agree that people are at the foundation of any planning effort.

People are the cause for planning and, for the most part, the effect of planning, and the successes of those efforts are determined by how the results affect people. In order to understand how our communities will be shaped in the future, we must understand the people who will be affected by societal change. This is why the issue of migration and misplacement of African American populations is such an important consideration at the turn of the century, especially if we are to fully understand how African American lives will be subsequently shaped.

The need for population analysis became more crystallized in the 1960s with the explicit experiences of population shift. These shifts affected not only minority groups but others such as the elderly and children, and caused immediate changes in the nature and type of required research for understanding community growth. Data were needed not only from population studies but demographic analysis. Of course the Civil Rights Movement of the 1960s and the evolving legislative approaches and responses legitimized and intensified the need for accurate and a more telling demographic analysis. Therefore, African American migration has had a significant impact on the growth and planning of American cities and neighborhoods.

Housing

During the sixty years since the end of World War II, the number of housing units in the United States has grown by 150 percent, from 42 million in 1950 to 105 million in 2000. The proportion of total housing units that are owner occupied has also grown, from 43.6 to 66.2 percent. In 2012, the U.S. Census Bureau showed that the percentage of Black families who own their homes decreased between 2005 and 2012 from 46 percent. These figures, published in *BlackDemographics.com*, also present some very alarming statistics which appear to confirm the lack of progress by Blacks in the housing area despite years of struggle to equal the playing field. Incidentally, about 59.2 percent Blacks continue to rent and spend more than 30 percent of their income on rent, and there is a continuous decrease on their median gross rent and home value.[50]

The National Law Center estimates that at least 6.5 percent of the U.S. population has been homeless at one point, and in the next five years, more than seven million people are expected to be homeless. Given this gloomy picture, it is apparent that the Housing Act of 1949 that was intended to promote the provision of low-income housing did not yield measurable program results at least to the extent that subsequent problems with housing shortages were abated. This legislative strategy that was supported by Harry Truman was caught in the civil rights struggles; it failed to secure congressional support, thus adding to the ambiguity of Truman's support of the civil rights struggles.

As an indictment of the federal government, Milwaukee Mayor John Norquist decried in the 1998 book *The Wealth of Cities: Revitalizing the Centers of American Life* that the government "killed affordable housing" by choking "market mechanisms that would attract private investment." What are African Americans supposed to do when the playing field is not leveled? While the struggle for equality and fair and affordable housing continues for African Americans, it has taken almost fifty years since the Truman Housing Act was passed to see real progress in minority housing ownership.

In a report published by the Clinton White House in August 2000, the government released its grip on several economic mechanisms that would support housing ownership.[51] With an anticipated surplus of $211 billion, the National Economic Council reported the addition of

50 James H. Carr, et al. "The state of the US Economy and Homeownership for African Americans," *The State of Housing in Black America 2013*. Lanham, CA: The National Association of Real Estate Brokers (NAREB). http://Blackdemographics.com/households/housing/, retrieved May 12, 2014.

51 John O. Norquist (1998). *The Wealth of Cities: Revitalizing the Centers of American Life*, Cambridge, MA: Perseus Publishing. (For a detailed and insightful discussion of the housing condition for Blacks in the United States.)

a million new jobs to the economy since 1993, and African American unemployment hit a record low, falling from 14.2 percent in 1992 to an average 7.7 percent in 2000. There was also an increase of 7.7 percent in one-year median income for African American families with real wages rising to 8.2 percent in three years. These positive economic indicators and results spurred the highest homeownership among African Americans on record.

Between 1994 and 1999, the number of African American families who owned their own homes increased by 1.1 million. But in making projections about sustainable growth in the housing sector for African Americans and their ability to own single-family homes, problems still abound. Recent reports from the Bush administration in the housing area are not encouraging. In fact, in the first four years of the Bush administration (2001–2004), the Bureau of Labor Statistics reported that the U.S. economy lost 1.6 million jobs. The African American unemployment rate stood at 10.4 percent in August 2004, an increase of 27 percent since President Bush had taken office.

The aforementioned unemployment rate is above the national average. The White population unemployment rate is reported to be 4.7 percent. The Census Bureau also reported that the amount African Americans earned per each dollar "fell from sixty-five cents in 2000 to sixty-two cents in 2003, and nearly one in four African Americans lives in poverty. In 2000 the African American poverty rate reached a record low of 22.5 percent. These falling incomes and high unemployment rate among African Americans caused an 8.4 percent rise in the poverty rate in 2003. These figures suggest a reversal of the Clinton/Gore administration's policies,[52] and they negatively affect housing ownership among African Americans. In fact, the Census Bureau reports that the "Black home ownership gap has grown by 2–6 percent." How can African Americans achieve parity in home ownership when years of progress are reversed and economic indicators point in the wrong direction, especially for African Americans?

Poverty is not providence-endowed for African Americans. While most have the intention to struggle and raise their achievement level beyond that of their parents, lingering and continuous problems associated with classism, racism, and discrimination create an

---

[52] The Clinton-Gore Administration: A Record of Progress, published by the White House in August 2000.

institutionalized impediment to progress. Perhaps the one viable solution to these prohibitive impediments is to cast aside the conditionalities associated with homeownership that delimits the ability of many African Americans to qualify. These regulations are associated with credit structure, minimum income requirements, and issues of family size. Community-based organizations are often equipped with the knowledge about prevailing social milieu and can often introduce acceptable community interventions and corrective measures aimed at promoting and encouraging homeownership. In fact, according to Fannie Mae's 2003 National Homeownership Survey, many minorities of modest means and "other underserved" families often lack information associated with the process of homeownership.[53]

While some progress has been made recently by faith-based community organizations in many cities, much work still remains to be done. But this present discussion cannot end without addressing the often-debated issue that the decrease in Black homeownership is a consequence of the economy and the resulting foreclosure of many homes. But why are homes owned by Blacks and Hispanics disproportionately foreclosed? Evidence suggests that from 2007, when the foreclosure crisis was first documented, 8 percent of homes owned by both African Americans and Latinos were foreclosed as compared to 4.5 percent homes owned by non-Hispanic Whites, even with Non-Hispanic Whites holding the largest number of mortgages.[54] The housing market cannot be effectively rejuvenated when there is disparate treatment regarding who can stay in the market. The process consequentially becomes a revolving door.

---

[53] Fannie Mae, December 10, 2004, and Fannie Mae National Housing Survey 2003/New Release, April 2004.

[54] D. G. Bocian, W. Li, and K. S. Ernst (2010). "Foreclosures by Race and Ethnicity: The Demographics of a Crisis," Durham, NC: Center for Responsible Lending. http://www.responsiblelending.org.mortgage-lending/research-analysis/foreclosures-by-race-and-ethnicity.pdf, retrieved May 27, 2014.

Chapter 5

IS IT THE JUSTICE SYSTEM OR THE "JUST US" SYSTEM?

The periodical *Post-Secondary Education Opportunity* determined in 1996 that there were more Black males in prisons and jails than there were enrolled in college:

The focus of this celebration [Independence Day] invites a complacent belief that the vision of those who debated and compromised in Philadelphia yielded the "more perfect union" it is said we now enjoy.

I cannot accept this invitation, for I do not believe that the meaning of the Constitution was forever "fixed" at the Philadelphia Convention. Nor do I find the wisdom, foresight, and sense of justice exhibited by the Framers particularly profound. To the contrary, the government they devised was defective from the start, requiring several amendments, a civil war, and momentous social transformation to attain the system of constitutional government, and its respect for the individual freedoms and human rights, we hold as fundamental today. When contemporary Americans cite "the Constitution," they invoke a concept that is vastly different from what the Framers barely began to construct two centuries ago.

—Former Supreme Court Justice Thurgood Marshall

"According to the US Bureau of Justice Statistics, non-Hispanic Blacks accounted for 39.4 percent of the total prison and jail population in 2009 (841,000 Black males and 64,800 Black females out of a total of 2,096,300 males and 201,200 females). According to the 2010 census of the US Census Bureau, Blacks (including Hispanic Blacks) comprised 13.6 percent of the US population."[55]

Perhaps even more alarming, according to the Bureau of Justice Statistics, is the fact that "In 2010, Black non-Hispanic males were incarcerated at the rate of

---

[55] Overview of Race and Hispanic Origin: 2010 Census Briefs. US Census Bureau. See Tables 1 and 2.

Black population. Annual Social and Economic (ASEC) Supplement to the Current Population Survey (CPS). US Census Bureau.[dead link] "B02001. RACE—Universe: TOTAL POPULATION." 2009 American Community Survey 1-Year Estimates. United States Census Bureau. Retrieved October 24, 2014.

4,347 inmates per 100,000 US residents of the same race and gender. White males were incarcerated at the rate of 678 inmates per 100,000 US residents. Hispanic males were incarcerated at the rate of 1,755 inmates per 100,000 US residents."[56]

In 2013, by age eighteen, 30 percent of Black males, 26 percent of Hispanic males, and 22 percent of White males were arrested. By age twenty-three, 49 percent of Black males, 44 percent of Hispanic males, and 38 percent of White males were arrested.[57]

Young Black males are much more likely to be arrested and imprisoned as juvenile offenders than are Whites. Although Blacks make up about 12 percent of the U.S. population, they constituted 60.1 percent of juvenile felony defendants in a survey of forty large cities. As of midyear 2003, according to the Bureau of Justice Statistics, "an estimated 12 percent of Black males, 3.7 percent of Hispanic males, and 1.6 percent of Whites in their twenties were in prison or jail."

In fact, legal scholar and rights advocate Michelle Alexander posits that incarceration of Black youth is the "new Jim Crow," which is, according to her, designed to keep Black youth of voting age from the polls. She further contends that there are "more African Americans under prison control, on probation, or on parole than were enslaved in 1850, a decade before the Civil War began."[58]

Since 1950, the number of federal and state prisoners has grown from 166,123 to 1,345,842, a 710 percent increase. Violent crime in the United States remained close to two-decade lows, but the murder rate was higher than in virtually all other developed countries, according to FBI data as reported by the *Agence France-Presse* in 2013. The FBI also reported a rise in violent crimes to 0.7 percent in 2012 from 2011, while property crime fell by 0.9 percent. The bureau explained that these figures showed a decline in crime activities in the United States since 1993.

---

[56]   Bennett, Hans (October 22, 2009). "Book Review: Asian-American Prisoners," ColorLines.com. Retrieved May 27, 2014

[57]   Simon McCormack. "Nearly Half of Black Males, 40 Percent of White Males Are Arrested by Age 23: Study," Huffingtonpost.com. Retrieved May 27, 2014.

[58]   Michelle Alexander (2012). "How Mass Incarceration Turns People of Color into Permanent Second-Class Citizens," *The New Jim Crow: Mass Incarceration in the Age of Colorblindness*. New York, NY: New Press.

But what does that really mean in light of the recent declaration by the United Nations that the United States has the highest crime rate in the world? Some intelligence and crime experts seem to think the decrease is due to the corresponding decrease of drug use by Americans. But an FBI survey showed that "14,827 people were murdered last year in the United States, well down from 24,526 in 1993, when the country's population was smaller. But the 2012 murder rate—4.7 murders per 100,000 people—was significantly higher than in most other wealthy nations."[59] The comparable murder rate is 0.4 in Japan, 0.8 in Germany, 1.0 in Australia, 1.1 in France, and 1.2 in Britain, according to figures compiled by the Organization for Economic Cooperation and Development.[60]

Adult and Juvenile Crime

While crime is intolerable in a society, its origins and causes reflect social conditions as well as individual values. The fact that Blacks in America are much more likely to experience incarceration than Whites or other ethnic minorities, principally Hispanics, could possibly be symptomatic of lingering racial intolerance that has been endemic in American society for most of its history.

The link between educational attainment and incarceration is clear from data collected from the Survey of Inmates in State and Federal Correctional Facilities, 1997 and 1991, and the Survey of Adults on Probation, 1995, both of which are compiled by the Bureau of Justice Statistics. Almost two-fifths (39.7 percent) of state prisoners and 46.5 percent of local jail inmates lack a high school diploma, rates far below the attainment levels of the general population, in which 18.4 percent lack high school education.

Many prisoners are incarcerated, at least in part, because of a disability. According to the Bureau of Justice Statistics, almost threefifths (59 percent) of state prisoners with less than a high school education had a speech disability, while two-thirds (66 percent) had a learning disability. Of all state prison inmates, 16.1 percent had a mental condition, 11.9

---

[59]   *The Raw Story*, "US murder rate higher than nearly all other developing nations: FBI data," *Agence France-Presse*, September 16, 2013, retrieved May 27, 2014.

[60]   Ibid.

percent had a limiting physical condition, 9.8 percent had a learning disability, and 3.7 percent had a speech disability. Presented with the opportunity to improve their education, more than half (52 percent) of the state prison population reported taking education courses. Most of these prisoners took GED or vocational courses.

More than one-third (34.9 percent) of local jail inmates listed behavioral or academic problems or lack of interest as reasons they had dropped out of school, while a sample of the general population interviewed reported these reasons about half that often (17.2 percent).

Although much public debate about law enforcement and sentencing portrays those convicted of crimes as "career criminals," most inmates reported having a job before they were arrested. The proportion of inmates with former full-time or part-time jobs ranged from 62.5 percent for those without a high school education to 78 percent for those with some college. Most inmates reported wage income of less than $1,000 a month. Although most inmates were employed before arrest, their unemployment rate was also much higher than for the general population. Less-educated inmates were more likely to have lower income than were better-educated inmates. About one-tenth of all inmates reported to have experienced homelessness at some time within twelve months of their arrest.[61]

According to the FBI, 75.8 percent of juvenile arrests were for drug-related offenses in 1998. This represents an increase from 1980, when 51.2 percent of juvenile arrests were so categorized. Most drug-related arrests were connected with marijuana possession (74.4 percent in 1980 and 61.8 percent in 1998).

Some argue that the sharp rise in drug arrests is more a reflection of much tougher law enforcement and sentencing practices than an actual increase in drug use. But tougher law enforcement for drug-related offences is needed if society is to rid itself of illegal drug activity and other social maladies. These issues are sensitive and subject to interpretation. However, one thing is clear: Society needs fair and equitable application of public policies and enforcement of the law.

The article "Treatment versus Incarceration," written by Dough McVey and others, and published by the *Justice Policy Institute* in 2004, summarizes the ways in which the criminal justice system creates racial

---

[61] See the National Archives of Criminal Justice data: http://www.icpsr.umich. edu/icpsrweb/content/NACJD/guides/sisfcf.html. Retrieved May 27, 2014.

disparity in juvenile drug cases: Although White youth sell and use drugs at the same or higher rates as youth of color, Black and Latino youth are arrested, prosecuted, and imprisoned at dramatically higher rates for drug crimes. McVey et al. also provide a compelling discussion as to why treatment for substance abuse is preferred to incarceration. As a compendium to this assessment, Manning Marable writes in the *Journal for Social and Environmental Justice* an article titled "Incarceration versus Education: Reproducing Racism and Poverty in America." He states, "There is overwhelming evidence that the overrepresentation of Blacks in prisons is largely due to discrimination in every phase of the criminal justice system. ... according to the 2007 ACLU study, for example, African Americans comprised 11 percent of Texas' population but 40 percent of the state's prisoners. Blacks in Texas are incarcerated at roughly five times the rate of Whites. Despite the fact that Blacks statistically represent fewer than 10 percent of drug abusers, in Texas 50 percent of all prisoners incarcerated in state prisons and two-thirds of all those in jails for 'drug-delivery offenses' are African Americans."[62]

Among young people incarcerated in juvenile facilities for the first time on a drug charge, the rate of persistence among Black youths is forty-eight times that of Whites, while the rate for Latino youths is thirteen times that of Whites. Black youths are three times more likely than White youths to be admitted to an adult prison for a drug conviction. While the rate of young Whites being sent to prison for drug offenses from 1986–96 doubled, the comparable Black rate increased sixfold.[63]

Whether or not the consequences of the street-level war on drugs are intended by policymakers, the effects are devastating. Inmates' lives are interrupted and often change direction entirely. Their children are for years without a parent (56 percent of inmates in 1999 left children younger than eighteen behind). Potentially productive people are removed from the population and from the support of their families. Former inmates are deprived of the right to vote. It has been estimated

---

[62] For a thorough analysis of the argument, see Manning Marable's article "Incarceration versus Education: Reproducing Racism and Poverty in America" in the *Journal of Social and Environmental Justice-Race and Regionalism*, Vol. 15, No. 1, Fall 2008.

[63] "Incarceration versus Education," The Drug Policy Alliance, retrieved May 27, 2014. http://www.drugpolicy.org/.

that some 1.4 million Black men, or 13 percent of the Black male adult population, have been disenfranchised.

To thoroughly answer or debate the question of disparate treatment of minorities in matters related to substance abuse or the peddling of illegal drugs, one must visit the scene of the crime. American policies and policymakers take their cues from the Constitution. It sets, or at least is expected to set, the stage and provide a frame of reference for all related policy matters. Therefore, to seek answers to mind-boggling questions by looking to the U.S. Constitution is not completely unreasonable. In attempting to resolve the issue of establishing equity and fairness in representation, the framers of the Constitution recognized African slaves as property that must be counted in order to determine representation by States. Southern Whites, with their large slave ownership, wanted slaves to be counted as whole persons, while northern Whites did not see the inclusion of slaves as part of the population as being necessary. In a compromise, it is written into Article I, Section 2, paragraph 3, "Representation and direct taxes shall be apportioned among the several states, which may be included within the Union, according to their respective numbers, which shall be determined by adding to the whole number of free persons, including those bound to service for a term of years and excluding Indians not taxed, three-fifths of all other persons."

Perhaps the counting of a Negro as three-fifths of a person provides us with the psychological underpinning for uncovering the reason why the contributions of African Americans to the American society are minimized. The Constitution of the United States clearly and demonstrably explains the quandary. Today, many people in society still view African Americans as three-fifths of a person; this explains why the most uneducated White believes he or she is more of a human than the most educated African American regardless of whether that education was obtained from an Ivy League institution.

Those who wish to challenge this thinking must first challenge the language of the Constitution and the many real cases and stories of crimes committed against African Americans, most of which are racially motivated. When law enforcement officers target African Americans because they believe this group is more likely to engage in criminal activity, there is a racially motivated overtone. How did the law enforcement community arrive at that conclusion? Is it because African Americans are seen as inferior and not capable of positive accomplishments? Sounds familiar, does it not? In fact, while racial profiling is prima facie illegal, private property, especially certain types of automobile, are often stopped for traffic violations when there is reason to believe that such an automobile may be used for drug or illegal weapon trafficking. When drugs or weapons are discovered in these automobiles, the court usually rules in favor of the prosecution, and subsequently, this court ruling is often used as a justification for targeting African Americans and making regular arrests.

Both the federal, state, and local courts take their cue from the Supreme Court; therefore, cases that border on this legal precedent receive similar treatment and often yield comparable results because the Constitution demeaned African Americans in Article I when it defined them as a fraction of a person. African Americans are regularly seen as inferior and are arrested and incarcerated because their actions are often viewed as being naturally complementary to their constitutionally established legal status.

Many instances of racial profiling have been highlighted recently. While Section 1 of the Fourteenth Amendment to the United States constitution guarantees all Americans equal treatment under the law, the American Civil Liberties Union (ACLU) continues to litigate cases of racial profiling across the nation. On March 3, 1991, Rodney King, who was driving with two friends, was stopped by the Los Angeles police department (LAPD) officers following a high-speed chase on the 210 freeway with the California Highway Patrol. King reportedly had been drinking with his friends. Ordered out of car, King was repeatedly beaten and kicked by officers, even while he was in handcuffs. The four White police officers involved in the beating claimed self-defense and were later acquitted of any crime. This incident set off massive rioting, burning and looting by King's supporters. The Rodney King case in 1991 in Los Angeles is still vividly clear in our minds. Several other racially motivated crimes against African Americans have been committed over the years, including James Byrd, Jr. of Jasper County, Texas, who was dragged for two and a half miles to his death after his throat had been cut.

Sam Torres's article "Hate Crimes against African Americans" in the *Journal of Contemporary Criminal Justice* provides statistics from the FBI's uniform crime report on hate crimes, which show that African Americans are most often victims of racially motivated crimes. It is clear that from 1992 to 1996, the number of hate crimes reported against African Americans increased by about 52 percent.[64]

However, on balance, it is necessary to point out that other ethnic minorities and poor Whites have also been victims of racially motivated crimes but with differences in motivation and procedure for arrests.

Preacher, Save Thyself

The criminal activity against African Americans has been pervasive, and the regular arrests of African Americans--young and old, male and female--have become a common occurrence in our society. The ACLU, the NAACP, and other organizations are at the forefront of the struggle to challenge policies aimed at strengthening the penal system and its outright assault on African American youth. Individual efforts in the African American communities are also noticeable. Scholars such as Cornel West, in his works *Race Matters* (2000) and *Keeping Faith* (1993), and Henry Louis Gates, Jr., in editing the collection *"Race," Writing, and Difference* (1992), have provided particularly powerful messages about racism and the African American predicament in the United States. These scholars, as well as others before them, have received their own share of criticism and challenges, but they have been steadfast in their delivery. Apparently, they still believe in the proper education of the "Negro."

A cacophony of progressive voices continues to emerge from African American communities either in condemnation of the policies that continue to ensure the increasing arrest of African Americans or in support of African American education for change. Besides the known voices of the Civil Rights Movement, such as the Rev. Jesse Jackson; Rev. Joseph Lowry; Rev. Andrew Young; Rep. Eleanor Holmes Norton; Rev. Dr. E. Gail Anderson Holness; and others, many new voices in the African American communities have taken a stand against racially motivated arrests and incarceration.

Despite these goodwill efforts, many African Americans have unintentionally fed the system that seeks to destroy them, and in doing

---

[64]   Sam Torres (1999). "Hate Crimes against African Americans: The Extent of the Problem," *Journal of Journal of Contemporary Criminal Justice*, Vol. 15, No. 1, 48–63.

so, they have perhaps sold their souls for money. The "artists"—such as rappers and others—portray a gang mentality, East against West, North against South, and "get-rich-quick" schemes that deprive us of self-respect and feed into the psychologically inferior profile that was first established by the Constitution of the United States. Remember, the Constitution defined Blacks as a fraction of a human being and tolerated Jim Crow laws with demeaning conditions, thus prohibiting Blacks from participating in the political process. Attitudes and social behaviors must be changed if society is to respect African American efforts.

Chapter 6

HEALTHCARE IS NOT FOR THOSE WHO NEED IT MOST: HEALTH DISPARITIES

Disease occurs under human circumstances such as housing conditions and educational opportunities. … Providing all Americans with comparable access to such opportunities in addition to health-care may reduce the uneven burden of disease. —Harold Freeman, president and CEO, North General Hospital, panelist at the Future of Public Health Millennial Symposium Series (Harvard School of Public Health) discussing "Reducing Inequalities in Health Outcomes in the United States," February 23, 2001.

Historic and current racial inequality has had an obvious impact on the comparative health and longevity of Blacks. Disparities are partially due to economic and environmental factors as well as access barriers.

The affluent citizens of this nation enjoy better health than do its minority and poorer citizens. The more striking health disparities involve shorter life expectancy among the poor, and higher rates of cancer, birth defects, infant mortality, asthma, diabetes, and cardiovascular disease. Although health-care access might account for some of this disparity, the differences in environmental and occupational exposures are also thought to play a role. Minority and poorer communities are more likely to live in polluted environments and to work in hazardous occupations. The environmental justice literature is inundated with stories about communities that are often faced with the possibility of a hazardous waste material facility being established in their area.

The resistance to such action is often followed by the verbal reaction "not in my backyard." This sort of reaction has been called the "NIMBY principle" by environmental groups. In fact, in 1983, the NAACP argued against the placement of a hazardous waste landfill in a Black neighborhood and called it "environmental racism" following a study conducted by the United Church of Christ, which concluded that "race is the most significant factor in determining the location of hazardous waste facilities."[65] In fact, according to Roberta Crowell Barbalace in *Environmental Justice* and the NIMBY principle, "Some hazardous waste companies have contended that they do not 'target minority neighborhoods.'" Others, such as Waste Management, accept the premise that for whatever reason, there is a disproportional distribution of environmental assets and liabilities among racial groups, minorities, and economically depressed communities."[66]

Assessments such as the one presented above can be used to explain why even as health-care technology has improved longevity, throughout the past fifty years the age-adjusted death rate in the Black population has remained substantially higher than that of Whites and other racial and ethnic groups. In 1950, the overall death rate for Blacks was 1,722.1 per 100,000 population, or 22.1 percent above the rate for Whites (1,410.8). By 2000, the death rate among Blacks had fallen to 121.4, or 32 percent higher than the death rate for Whites.

Life expectancy increased for both Whites and Blacks since 1950. Blacks born in 1950 on the average could expect to live to 60.8 years, while Whites born then had a life expectancy of 69.1 years, a disparity of 8.3 percent. Blacks born in 2000 can expect to live to 72.2 years, while Whites born in 2000 can expect 77.6 years of life, a disparity of 7.9 percent, or a relative improvement. Data such as these are telling signs of serious health disparities in African American populations.

In 2002, the U.S. Department of Health and Human Services (HHS) identified six focus areas where serious health disparities exist, both in health delivery, access, and outcome. The areas and their relevant statistics are:

---

[65] Robert Bullard, John Lewis, and Benjamin Chavis (1994). *Unequal Protection: Environmental Justice and Communities of Color,* San Francisco, CA: Sierra Club Books.

[66] http://environmentalchemistry.com/yogi/hazmaUarticles/nimby.html.

1. Infant mortality: African Americans and other ethnic minorities have higher death rates than Whites. African American death rates jumped to 5 percent for 2000 from 2.4 in 1998. This, according to HHS, is a decade-long trend.

2. In cancer screening and management, African American women are more likely to die of cervical cancer than White women and more likely to die of breast cancer than any other ethnic group minority.

3. In 2000, although minorities are more likely than whites to be diagnosed with diabetes, ... the rate of diabetic ESRD is 2.6 times higher among African Americans than any other group.

4. Although African Americans and Hispanics represented only 26 percent of the population in 2001 based on U.S. census figures, they accounted for 66 percent of all adult HIV/AIDS cases and 82 percent of all pediatric cases that were reported during the first half of 2001.

5. The death rate from cardiovascular diseases among African Americans was 29 percent higher in 2000, and for stroke, their death rate was 40 percent higher than that of Whites.

6. In 2001, African Americans sixty-five or older were less likely to receive influenza or pneumonia vaccines.[67] The Centers for Disease Control (CDC) admitted in its June 29, 2001, 50 (25): 532-7 weekly report that racial/ethnic disparities continued in vaccination levels from 1997 to 1999. Influenza vaccination levels were lower among persons with less than a high school education or between the ages of 65 to 74 than among persons with higher education levels or older age.

In addition to these areas, disparities also exist in other important aspects of health, including mental health, hepatitis, syphilis, and tuberculosis. Karen Williams and Veronica Johnson write in the *Harvard Health Policy Review*, "The legacy of racial and ethnic disparities suffered by African Americans (the second largest minority group in the United States) consistently reminds patients, health practitioners, and policymakers of the taint of America's 'slave health deficit.' Infamous

---

[67] National Center for Health Statistics (NCHS), 2002 National Center for Chronic Disease Prevention and Health Promotion; 2000 U..S. Department of Health and Human Services.

health scandals like the Tuskegee syphilis study affect the health-care choices of both Blacks and their providers, often against a backdrop of racists', classists' and paternalists' medical conduct."[68]

This assessment by Williams and Johnson is very instructive of the nature and magnitude of the problem, especially when grounded in historical analysis. Disparities in healthcare for African Americans exist beyond care; it is at the core of the type of care they receive. This link between disparity in delivery and care was justified by a Kaiser Foundation study that showed that about 77 percent of minority or African American people believed in this assessment.[69]

In the past, studies of the patterns of health-care provision have often emphasized equity in delivery. Recently, based on overwhelming evidence in literature and medical testimonials, the focus shifted from the notion of under-treatment seeking equity to that of equality. This paradigm shift corroborates the sentiments of the Kaiser study. African American patients are not convinced that the type of care they receive is equal to that received by their White counterparts. In fact, when discussions about health disparities among African Americans are moved from the metropolitan context to a rural setting, the issue of health-care disparity is even more deplorable.

In an examination of three Southern states, Georgia, Mississippi, and Alabama, where the African American population is high and rising, HIV/AIDS is used as a benchmark for analyzing disparity. In Georgia, the following data is discerned for African Americans: One out of two women with AIDS lives in rural Georgia, and AIDS cases among African Americans are eleven times, five times, and three times higher than among their Asian-Pacific Islander, American Indian/Alaskan Native, and Latino counterparts, respectively.[70] In Alabama, African American death rates from all causes are 25 percent higher than White death rates; African Americans are four times more likely to die from homicide, three times as likely to die of diabetes, prostate cancer, and cervical cancer, and twice as likely to die of asthma or kidney diseases. The data presented above are greater for African Americans than that

---

68   Karen Williams and Veronica Johnson. "African American Health Disparity via History-Based Review," *Harvard Health Policy Review*, Vol. 3, No. 2, Fall 2002.

69   Ibid.

70   Georgia Minority Health and Health Disparity Report; Morehouse School of Medicine Primary Care.

for Whites in all age groups except those eighty-five years and older. Also, African Americans are at greater risk of being victimized through sexually transmitted diseases such as HIV/AIDS.[71]

This Alabama Rural Health Report suggests adjustments in policies related to environmental factors, health insurance, education, transportation, and stress, all of which the report categorizes as access barriers. In Mississippi, African Americans comprise 37 percent of the population but account for about 75 percent of all reported HIV/AIDS cases; premature infant deaths are 1.5 times greater for African Americans than for Whites; infant mortality rates are two times greater for African Americans than for Whites; and the incidence of diabetes is two times greater among African Americans than among Whites.[72] Part of the problem is blamed on sporadic visits to physicians, poor rural healthcare, and environmental health issues. In all three states, the overriding reason for the disparity appears to be a high illiteracy rate, especially in the area of health and poverty. African Americans continue to be disproportionately educated, especially in the South, and as long as the trend continues, disparities in health and other areas will continue to exist.

Moreover, a corresponding report by the Rural Healthy People 2010, edited by Larry D. Gamm, et al. of the Southwest Rural Health Research Center at Texas A&M University Science Center's School of Rural Public health, corroborates several other independent studies by indicating that there are more serious health problems in rural than urban centers, and many rural areas lack access to professionals and/or health insurance for addressing health problems.[73]

In all cases, suggested strategies for corrective action include education, both general and health-specific, and increased advocacy on the part of state and local governments, including personal responsibilities related to behavioral changes and personal choices. While it is suggestive to view education and/or a lack thereof as being the primary reason why many poor people do not seek healthcare, the literature on health disparity overwhelmingly supports the notion

---

[71]   "Failing a Crisis," December 2002. Clyde Bargainer, Alabama Rural Health Report, Vol. 3, No. 1, March 2003.

[72]   Eliminating Health Disparities Focusing on Mississippi, 2004, www.Apha.org/ NPHW/pressroom/Mississippi_facts_letter.pdf

[73]   http://sph.tamhsc.edu/centers/rhp2010/Volume2.pdf.

that access or equal access to healthcare is more of a determinant to utilization than education.

In fact, in a paper by Dubay, Holahan, and Cook (2006), the research indicates that "nearly two-fifths of adults who lacked health insurance for a year or more reported not being able to see a physician when needed in the past year due to cost, and nearly 70 percent of those in fair or poor health reported such barriers. These barriers were greatest for women, Blacks, the unemployed, and those with low incomes. Long-term uninsured adults were much less likely to receive mammography, pap smears, colon cancer screening, and hypertension and cholesterol screenings."[74]

Implications for Public Policy

It is evident that the many meaningful improvements in the conditions of Black American life still leave substantial inequality. Despite the continuing progress by highly talented and visible Blacks who are breaking down individual barriers, the great majority of Blacks in the United States remain in an unfavorable position, less likely than others to acquire the benefits of living in the most powerful country in the world. In some facets of public life, the gaps between the races are narrowing, while in other respects the gaps remain unchanged or are even worse than they were before.

The "war on poverty," once a bold new public program, evolved into a system that employed many upwardly mobile Blacks and Hispanics and sympathetic Whites. Rather than conferring real economic power and assets on Black and Hispanic communities and the poor within them, poverty programs largely operated in a paternalistic mode, providing at best a "hand up" that would help the most persistent individuals gain access to opportunities previously forbidden and allow them to take a place in mainstream corporate America.

Where once-popular protests against blatant abuses and soaring oratory commanded the nation's attention, the issues of inequality are far less dramatic and personalized, more obscured and complicated, and

---

[74] Dubay, Lisa, John Holahan, and Allison Cook, "The Uninsured And The Affordability Of Health Insurance Coverage," Health Affairs (Web Exclusive), November 2006, doi:10.1377/hlthaff.26.1.w22. Accessed August 13, 2014.

political action is more difficult. In 1963, the symbols of White resistance were once individuals such as George Wallace and Bull Connor, who could easily be characterized as "evil" or at least misguided. Now forty years later, the enemy of true equality is more likely to be the fine print in a piece of legislation or the bias built into questions on a standardized gate-keeping test. We know healthcare is but one aspect of the problem.

Even as more African Americans than ever before acquire a greater stake in the status quo, few have real power. Those who are close to the seat of power, such as Dr. Condoleezza Rice, are either limited by the highly political nature of their jobs as presidential appointees hired to help carry out policies or toe the political line. They exhibit an indifferent attitude to the problem and see African American problems not as a racially specific predicament but as America's problem, thus undermining its importance to the body politic.

There is still an alienated, powerless group at the bottom in inner cities and rural areas for whom there has been little but symbolic improvement in the past fifty years. Many members of this group have been through one or more social programs without being able to change their circumstances, mainly because benefits derived from social programs are fixed, so they rarely keep pace with cost-of-living or inflationary trends. Social benefits are merely for sustenance; there are no excesses, hence no savings. The resulting circumstance is continuous dependence on a system that barely provides living wages. It presents a revolving door of poverty. In an increasingly conservative and prosperous America, the mass media pay little attention to such unglamorous problems. Concentration of economic power and continuing corporate welfare threaten to make the powers of the growing numbers of African American-elected officials and their White, Hispanic and Asian counterparts more and more irrelevant in determining the nation's future and its response to issues of inequality.

Chapter 7

HEALTH-CARE REFORM AND DISPARITIES IN AMERICA

Obamacare will destroy the greatest health care system the world has ever known.—Senator Jeff Sessions (R), Alabama

Historical Perspective

A discussion on health reform and disparities in the United States cannot take place without first documenting the historical movement for implementing universal health-care coverage for Americans.

The demand for universal healthcare in the United States has been likened historically to many other social movements, including women's protests, labor uprisings, age-related laws, and welfare reforms to address poverty issues. These reform movements were necessary at the dawn of the twentieth century as a grass-roots effort aimed at ensuring that many Americans were not marginalized and could realize the American dream.[75] Political analysts surmise that the reform movement in the United States occurred in the form of progressivism, which had a major influence in Europe and in the United States.[76]

The progressive movement was a response to modernization that witnessed the growth of the American industrial base, the expansion of railway networks, and the growth of American corporations; progressives were welcoming the ideas that established the focus of American politics

---

[75] Hoffman, Beatrix. "Health-Care Reform and Social Movement in the United States," *American Journal of Public Health*, A3 (1): 75-85, 2003.

[76] Derickson, Alan (2005). *Health Security for All: Dreams of Universal Health Care in America*, Baltimore: Johns Hopkins University Press.

and espoused social justice.[77] In fact, following these social sentiments, political candidates who promoted social issues were often supported by grass-roots movements. In 1912, Theodore Roosevelt was defeated in his presidential bid after he campaigned, unsuccessfully, for sickness insurance to be guaranteed by the state.[78] Due to industrial expansion, it became necessary to implement what was then called "industrial sickness insurance." Employees could purchase sickness insurance through employer-based funds.[79]

Other universal health initiatives were also prominent from the 1930s through the '50s. For example, President Truman defended a proposal for a national health insurance program for all Americans. In 1933, Franklin Roosevelt included a provision for a publicly funded health-care program as part of his social security legislation. In addition to these early presidential efforts, even the Congress of the United States passed legislation that favored third-party insurers. Private insurance such as Blue Shield—a physician group—began to sell health insurance policies to employers. In fact, after World War II, nonprofit organizations such as Kaiser Permanente offered fee-for-care to construction workers.[80]

Following is a catalog of selected prominent efforts aimed at insuring and providing universal health-care coverage to all Americans.

---

[77]   Harriby, Alonzo L. "Progressivism: A Century of Change and Rebirth," *Progressivism and the New Democracy*, Sidney M. Milkis and Jerome M. Mileur, eds. University of Massachusetts Press, 1999.

[78]   Walker, Forrest A. (Winter 1979). "Americanism versus Sovietism: A Study of the Reaction to the Committee on the Costs of Medical Care," *Bulletin of the History of Medicine* 53 (4): PMID 397839, 489–504.

[79]   Murray, John E. (2007). *Origins of American Health Insurance: A History of Industrial Sickness Funds*. New Haven, CT: Yale University Press.

[80]   Truman, Harry S. "Letter from Harry S. Truman to Ben Turoff," College Park, MD: National Archives and Records Administration, April 12, 1949. Retrieved December 2, 2011.

Period	Health Insurance Efforts
1965	Medicare insurance coverage for persons sixty-five or older. Signed into law by President Lyndon B. Johnson.
1970	Proposal for bipartisan national health insurance bill by Senator Edward Kennedy.
1972	President Richard Nixon signed the Social Security Amendment that extended Medicare to those sixty-five and younger with disabilities.
1974	President Gerald Ford called for health insurance reform.
1985	The consolidated Omnibus Budget Reconciliation Act amended ERISA (Employee Retirement Income Security Act) to allow employees to continue health-insurance coverage even after terminating employment.

Presidents Bill Clinton's and George H. W. Bush's health-insurance proposals and debates were often contentious and for the most part yielded limited or no results. In fact, the "Patients'" Bill of Rights that would have given consumers rights to their healthcare was similar to the Consumer Bill of Rights. On March 15, 1962, President John F. Kennedy presented a speech to the United States Congress in which he extolled four basic consumer rights, later called the Consumer Bill of Rights. These included consumer rights to safety, information choice, and the right to complain and be heard. A similar approach would apply to the Clinton/ Bush health-care initiative. Viewing this as the impending implications from standardizing healthcare caused an uproar in the medical environment. In fact, the American Medical Association (AMA) and the pharmaceutical industry unequivocally opposed any suggestion aimed at providing emergency care to anyone and/or authorizing patients to hold their health-care providers accountable for the nature and category of care.

Of course in 2003, President George Bush signed into law the Medicare Prescription Drug Improvement and Modernization Act for elderly and disabled Americans. This was seen as the largest revision of the Medicare Public Health program in thirty-eight years. Even with this gesture and comprehensive provisions, during the 2004 presidential election, George Bush and candidate John Kerry could not resolve the differences in their universal health-care proposals, at least not enough to gain acceptance from the medical community and other corporate entities that argued against universal health-care coverage.

In 2008, the Organization of Economic Cooperation and Development published the document "Economic Survey of the United States 2008: Health-Care Reform," in which it called for abolishing "employer-based insurance," among other things. That contention was immediately countered by a proposal by the Institute for America's Future that the government should offer a public health-insurance plan on a level playing field with private insurance plans.[81]

A New Era on Health-Care Reform

During the 2008 presidential election, the effort to reform health-care coverage and introduce universal applicability of care to the American public became a major policy argument. While Senator John McCain, the Republican presidential nominee, favored open-market competition rather than government funding for health care, Democratic presidential candidate Senator Barack Obama said universal healthcare would include "[t]he creation of the National Health Insurance Exchange that would include both private insurance plans and a Medicare–like, government-run option with coverage guaranteed regardless of health status or pre-existing conditions." The coverage would be comprehensive to include children (Leys 2008). Interestingly, an election poll retrieved in November 2008 found that for Obama's supporters, health-care concerns were their second priority, while for McCain's supporters, it was the fourth (Bleadon, et al. 2008). In this instance, it was clear that the issue of universal healthcare for America was based on party ideology. The battle lines on health-care policy were drawn.

In the ensuing month of the campaign, no solution on health-care reform issue was generated. After several town-hall meetings by members of Congress and the accompanying organized protest by members of the Tea Party, Republican members did not support a Senate bill on health-care reform. One would anticipate a political victory on this

---

[81]   Hickey, R., Jacob Hacker, and Pete Stark. "News Conference: The Case for Public Plan Choice in National Health Reform," Washington, D.C.: Institute for America's Future, December 17, 2008. Retrieved April 2, 2009.

matter for Obama, since winning the presidential election on a platform that included universal healthcare would be seen as a referendum, but that was not the case.

While states like Minnesota, Massachusetts, Vermont, and Connecticut had taken significant steps toward universal healthcare, other state-derived referendums failed in California in 1994 and Oregon in 2002. It is worth noting that even with the reluctance by states to pass the universal health-care law, the percentage of residents that are uninsured continues to rise. At 24 percent, Texas has the highest number of residents that are uninsured, followed by New Mexico at 22 percent. But with the upcoming looming and burgeoning number of U.S. residents without coverage, one would ask why there is so much opposition to affordable care.

Senator Jeff Sessions, a Republican from Alabama, issued a statement against Obama's health-care proposal. In it, he claimed that "Obamacare" was destroying "[t]he greatest health-care system the world has ever known" in addressing the U.S. Senate. Senator Sessions admitted that Americans die but still have the best health care in the world.[82] While some saw the senator's statement as horrible and arrogant, others simply took the high road by contending that the financial burden of the universal health-care system would be tremendous for a country that was still supporting the remnants of two military engagements in Iraq and Afghanistan.

But the World Health Organization ranks American healthcare thirty-second in the world (World Health Organization 2000). Also, the WHO points out that while America lags behind, countries such as Australia, Sweden, France, United Kingdom, Germany, the Netherlands, and Canada all have some form of universal health-care coverage for their citizens.

At Last: Obama's Affordable Care Act of 2010

The Patient Protection and Affordable Care Act (PPACA), commonly called Obamacare or the Affordable Care Act, was signed into law by President Barack Obama on March 23, 2010. Together with the

---

[82]   McAulliff, Michael. "Americans Die Sooner but Have Best Health Care in the World," *Huffington Post*, March 2, 2013.

health-care and education reconciliation act, Obamacare represents the most significant regulatory overhaul of the U.S. health-care system since Medicare and Medicaid in 1965.[83] Open enrollment commenced on March 31, 2014, after a protracted effort by congressional leaders to stall the statute, including a 2012 U.S. Supreme Court challenge and a ruling by the court in favor of the statute.

The statute has the following provisions: prohibit insurance companies from denying coverage to anyone with pre-existing conditions; mandate all citizens not covered by employer-provided health-care plans; provide health-insurance exchanges where individuals and small businesses can compare cost, coverage, and purchase policies; provide a sliding scale for coverage for persons with income between 100 and 400 percent of the federal poverty guidelines; expand Medicaid eligibility to all persons with income up to 133 percent of the federal poverty level; employee mandate for employers with fifty or more employees; and additional reforms to Medicare Part D coverage gap, commonly called the "donut hole," which is expected to shrink by 2020.[84]

Why Argue Against Affordable Care Act When Most Citizens Need Coverage?

Conservative political radio host and columnist Armstrong Williams published in the *Washington Times* on Sunday, October 27, 2013, an analysis/opinion titled "Why We Are Against Obamacare." In it, Williams postulates what he calls three basic arguments against the health-care statute. First, he argues that insurance premiums will not be as attractive as presented by those who support the act; second, there are price controls placed on the medical system in order to control the cost; and third, the act will negatively impact the economy by discouraging small businesses from expanding their employee poll beyond forty-nine. Other conservatives argue that because the act forces

---

[83] Vicini, J. and Jonathan Stempel. "Top court upholds health-care law in Obama triumph," *Reuters*, June 28, 2012.

[84] This is an annotated overview of the PPACA provisions. Complete and detailed information on the statute is available and published by the United States government printing office: Public Law 111/148 Patient Protection and Affordable Care Act, March 23, 2010.

citizens to participate in the health-care process, it violates contract law.[85] In addition to conservative political arguments against the act, the American College of Physicians (ACP) wrote letters in 2012, 2013, and 2014 to Medicare administrators, the U.S. Senate, and health and human services secretaries, contending that several provisions of the act should either be amended or repealed. [86]

While citizens continue to mount against the act, advocacy groups see the act as a solution to care denial to the poor and those with prolonged terminal illnesses. For example, the American Cancer Society praises the extension of care to children, touting the fact that because of preventive measures, the cancer society expects to see more cancer survivors.

In all, some Americans still hate Obamacare as a big government measure, but they simply like the fact that it will save millions of lives and provide benefits to most to overcome the sometimes insurmountable price tag associated with accessing care. It is simply a political paradox; therefore, as unattractive as it is for "big brother"—the government—to come to the rescue, Americans cannot stand the thought that they could not do it all by themselves. But who suffers in all this if "big brother" cannot help or is prohibited from helping? It will be the 3.1 million Americans who are too poor to purchase insurance but too old to stay on their parents' insurance. It is the 105 million Americans who cannot get care because of pre-existing conditions; it is the 6.1 million people on Medicare Part D who face the coverage gap; the 3.2 million small businesses who cannot afford to provide health insurance to their employees; the 4.34 million low-income citizens; the 50–129 million Americans who cannot get care because of their health conditions; and the 49.4 million who will have their Medicare benefits reduced or taken away. [87]

The seventeen million Americans who lacked some form of care and coverage before Obamacare demonstrate the disparities in health-care delivery in the United States. It appears that most Americans do not

---

[85]   Root, Damon. "The Best Legal Arguments against Obamacare," *Reason* magazine, March 24, 2012.

[86]   American College of Physicians (2013). *Affordable Care Act/Access to Care.* Philadelphia, PA., retrieved May 6, 2014.

[87]   Kohn, Susan. "317 Million Reasons to Love Obamacare," CNN opinion, March 31, 2014.

want the law repealed but as in any experiment or fledgling innovation, they prefer continuous monitoring for improvement.

Obamacare is not the only big social program that revolutionized the United States and faced tremendous opposition. Programs such as Social Security and welfare (including Medicaid and Medicare), and even the Civil Rights Movement experienced tremendous pushback, but today America seems to progressively embrace those constructs even with continuous arguments and proposals demanding changes. After all, this is the stuff that a true democracy is made of. There are many arguments about universal healthcare in a perfect or ideal democracy, but nevertheless we can accept the notion of "democratic ideals." The latter has its shortcomings and imperfections and can sometimes be antagonistic, but overall is the best practical system of government.[88]

---

[88]   Robert A. Dahl (1998). *On Democracy,* Connecticut: Yale University Press.

Chapter 8

SUMMARIZING THE CONDITION: ARE WE THERE YET?

Our lives begin to end the day we are silent about things that matter.—Martin Luther King, Jr.

To a great extent, domestic politics is the product of the ways in which disadvantaged individuals and communities respond to the struggle for survival. Crime, substance abuse, unemployment, poverty, teen pregnancy, racial conflict, domestic abuse, and family disintegration are all part of the legacy of racism.[89] The nation's response to these problems is often founded in a moralistic search for the best method of punishment rather than for effective methods of rehabilitation.[90]

Survival entails stress, both social and personal, and stress demands a response. How individuals respond to that stress (positively or negatively) might be seen as the genesis of many social and familial problems, from depression and rebellion and paranoia to domestic abuse, crime, and drug abuse. Whether the stress springs from an episode of unemployment, annoying behavior of another person, chronic failure in school, the inability to provide for one's family, or any of a multitude of daily or lasting setbacks, the stress of being African American in the United States is often a compelling force.

---

[89] For many of the profound statements, concerns, and quoted by Dr. Martin Luther King, Jr., I encourage you to read Clayborne Carson, ed. (2001). *The Autobiography of Martin Luther King Jr.*, New York, NY: Hachette Group.

[90] Additional discussion on the response by the government on the issues of hope in American can be gleaned from Martin Luther King, Jr., and James Melvin Washington, ed. (2003). *A Testament of Hope: The Essential Writings and Speeches of Martin Luther King, Jr.* (reprint edition), New York, NY: HarperOne.

Some responses to stress are socially accepted, such as prayer, the determination to try harder, or a single-minded focus on overcoming disadvantage through education, sports or music performance. Other responses are not socially accepted, and they are the focus of this chapter.

Racial Environment

Decades of racist images, practices, and political debate have assaulted the Black consciousness, all with the message that Blacks are unworthy of respect. Societal racism is bound to have a devastating impact on the self-esteem of an individual. Shared experiences of Blacks with harsh treatment by law enforcement, low expectations at school, discrimination in the workplace, and the sharp contrast between Black and White lifestyles and living conditions combined with societal racism create a corrosive atmosphere in which self-confidence and achievement are difficult to find.

The nature of racism has evolved from an open, blatant, and often legally enforced system of discrimination and segregation to a system in which opportunity is granted on the basis of place of residence, parents' educational attainment, and parental background. Racism shows up in a teacher's low expectations for children of poor and uneducated parents, a job interviewer's rating of an applicant's leadership qualities, a policeman's decision to look for crime in a Black neighborhood, or a banker's aversion to the investment in poor neighborhoods.

In recent years, there have been many television documentaries and print media materials regarding "redlining" in housing—where Blacks and other minorities have been directed to seek housing in some neighborhoods and not others. Even in the acquisition of permanent housing or other real estate, race-based decisions in the market is pervasive and well documented. Many companies in America have been caught with their hands in the cookie jar, and heavy penalties have been paid for racially based decisions and discrimination, including Denny's restaurant, Abercrombie and Fitch, Co., Adams Mark Hotel, and recently the Whirlpool Company.[91] Yet, denial of opportunity is often explained away as though it were based on reasons other than race.

Centuries of racism have engendered, in Darwinian fashion, an endurance and cultural stamina that somehow makes it possible for most Blacks in a community to lead constructive lives, and to raise children who do not rob and kill. Although there are more young African American males in jail than in college, there are still more young African American males who grow up in a low-income environment but do not go to jail.

Unfortunately, the response of the dominant White society to social problems is all too often grounded in resentment and punishment and in short-term fixes rather than in compassion or resolution of the problem.

Politics of Survival: Societal Trends and Individual Lives

More than a century and a half after the Emancipation Proclamation, Blacks in America are still twice as likely as Whites to be poor or unemployed, to grow up in a one-parent family, or to drop out of school. While some individuals have clearly benefited from affirmative action, recruitment by prestigious colleges, more equal opportunities in high-paying professions, and greater diversity in sports and entertainment, the majority of Blacks in America have remained disadvantaged in education, employment, health status, income, acquisition of homes and other assets, and most other areas.

These factors are all connected, especially in Black communities. Poor parents often have limited education and struggle to make ends meet. In school, their children often appear to teachers to have limited potential, perhaps because they are not dressed as neatly, or do not speak with the vocabulary and grammar, and may not perform with the same confidence that children from affluent families do. These children often react to teacher attitudes with poor academic performance and discipline

[91]   Bruckner, Tillett, Rossi, Cahill & Associates (2006). See also Justice Department Files Lawsuit against Adams' Mark Hotel Chain, December 16, 1999, www.usdoj.gov.

problems, and later they skip school and are more likely than children from non-poor families to drop out. Poverty and the lack of collective power and resolve appear to negatively affect one's ability to access basic social opportunities and achieve equity when receiving assistance.

Case in Point—Is It Class or Race? The 2005 New Orleans, Louisiana, Saga

In the early morning hours of August 29, 2005, a category 5 hurricane named Katrina swept through the Gulf Coast of the United States, with winds of 175 mph (280) km/h. This hurricane caused severe damage in Gulf Coast states, including Alabama, Mississippi, and Louisiana. In Louisiana, the storm surge caused the levee to break in New Orleans, flooding most of the city, which is below sea level. It caused widespread damage, evacuations, and deaths estimated to be in the thousands for its residence, who are predominantly African American and poor.

In a CBS news poll, 65 percent of Americans thought US President George W. Bush was too slow to respond to the disaster, and 58 percent disapproved of his performance. New Orleans Mayor Ray Nagin, who is African American, blamed Kathleen Blanco, the White Louisiana governor for the slow response, and collectively they blamed the bureaucracy and government red tape for the delayed response by state and federal officials for rescue efforts, food, and water for the predominantly displaced African American population. People were dying in the streets, and the shelters were overcrowded, and others clinked to rooftops in an effort to survive the rising water. Many more perished in the flood waters, all these within a twenty-four-hour period without any rescue attempts or other assistance. Observers pointed out that more than 80 percent of those who did not leave New Orleans before the flood were poor African Americans who could ill afford to leave. Others even alluded to the fact that even lighter skinned African Americans were hard to find among the crowd of all persons left behind, many of whom drowned and/or were separated from loved ones. Some blamed the lack of quick response and inept planning to the indifference of government planners about the welfare of poor African Americans. In short, the raging debate had been that wealthy and middle-class Whites and African Americans left New Orleans and the poor ones were to fend for themselves. What is your take? Is it race or class that determines who gets what, when, and how in "democratic" America?[92]

Since 1993, after Cornel West released his controversial yet thought-provoking book *Race Matters* and the ensuing debate immediately following that publication, several authors, academicians, and many media pundits appeared to conclude that the issue of race in America was put to rest.[93] Some even suggested that America had made such significant progress in its racial attitude that such debates were no longer necessary. In fact, others suggested that affirmative action as an instrument for creating racial parity should be eliminated in higher education and employment.

But in a landmark 2003 case involving the University of Michigan's affirmative action policies—one of the most important rulings on the issue in twenty-five years—the Supreme Court decisively upheld the right of affirmative action in higher education. Two cases, first tried in federal courts in 2000 and 2001, involved the University of Michigan's undergraduate program (*Gratz v. Bollinger*)[94] and its law school (*Grutter*

---

[92]   CNN News, February 27, 2006. Retrieved May 27, 2014. http://www.cnn. com/2006/US/02/27/katrina.poll/.

[93]   Cornel West (1993). *Race Matters,* Boston: MA, Beacon Press. I first read this classical work by Professor West when I was a newly minted PhD in political science from then Atlanta University. Professor West stimulated my interest in the politics of race as I witnessed around me the lucid yet controversial issues that he raised. I was challenged to examine the racial issues in America from an immigrant standpoint. I am glad I did. Yes, "race really still matters."

[94]   Supreme Court of the United States *Gratz et al. v. Bollinger et al.* Certiorari to the United States Court of Appeals for the Sixth Circuit.

v. Bollinger).[95] Other similar cases involve the University of Georgia, and the Ayers case in Mississippi.[96] In all, the court made it clear that affirmative action was still an important instrument for achieving racial parity, and that it is of great utility for policymakers. But despite such clear and eminent ruling, many in society still see race-based measures as unacceptable. Some still argue that America has achieved racial tolerance.

However, in the aftermath of Hurricane Katrina and the ensuing devastation in New Orleans, and after witnessing the apparent neglect of the poor, the elderly, and the mostly African American population, the same media that frowned at any suggestion of the prevalence of racial problems in America came full circle to confront its ghost. In fact, CNN reported, "Black residents of New Orleans were hit harder than their White counterparts by Hurricane Katrina, but they were also more likely to express optimism about the city's future, according to a poll released Monday. Fifty-three percent of Black respondents in the CNN/*USA Today*/Gallup poll reported they lost everything when Katrina slammed into the Gulf Coast August 29, compared with 19 percent of White respondents. And 52 percent of Whites said they were never separated from their loved ones, compared with 37 percent of Blacks. Twenty-six percent of Black respondents said they have been reunited after being separated from those they lived with; more than a third, 35 percent, said they were still separated."[97]

---

95   "Appeals Court Strikes down Michigan's Affirmative Action Ban," CNN News, retrieved from the www, November 19, 2012.

96   "The case was filed in 1975 by Jake Ayers, Sr., on behalf of his son and several other students attending Alcorn State University. A civil rights activist and former sharecropper, Ayers charged that Mississippi discriminated in its educational policies by offering a dual educational system for whites and blacks, with black schools, such as Alcorn, receiving inferior resources and facilities," from *Black Issues in Higher Education*, Vol. 18, No. 6. "The 1961 desegregation of the University of Georgia by Hamilton Holmes and Charlayne Hunter is considered a defining moment in civil rights history, leading to the desegregation of other institutions of higher education in Georgia and throughout the Deep South," The University of Georgia; 50 years of desegregation--2001 Holmes-Hunter lecture series.

97   CNN News, February 27, 2006. Retrieved from the www, May 27, 2014. http://www.cnn.com/2006/US/02/27/katrina.poll/.

This conclusion, therefore, suggests that responses to the aftermath of this event were based on race. Additionally, it may also provide the underlying premise why Blacks felt disenfranchised and why the government apparently responded slowly, given the limited number of Whites who were affected by the catastrophe.

Chapter 9

ECONOMIC PARITY AND FINANCIAL SECURITY OF AFRICAN AMERICANS DURING THE PAST FIFTY YEARS

In the Louisiana case that was previously cited, the following question has to be asked: Could the staggering number of African Americans who were displaced by the flood have been fewer if they had the same economic resources to flee from the city as their affluent counterparts?

We can assume it probably would have been the case, given our understanding of social mobility and the symmetrical relationship between social capital and access. Structural change in the U.S. economy and continued difficulty to access capital has undermined much of the African American economic ownership base in both farming and small business. On an individual level, the picture is mixed: a small but growing number of African Americans have succeeded in business, political, and professional careers, but a much larger number has stayed in place or moved backward, from relatively high-paying unionized jobs to service jobs with minimal pay and no benefits.

In the long term, the potential for Blacks to achieve economic parity and personal financial security is compromised by continued racism (now institutionalized) and an ever-weaker economic base in both the traditional small towns and rural communities of the South and inner-city communities outside the South.

Occupations

The numbers of college-educated, professional Blacks increased from 1940 to 1999. Teachers (except college level) were by far the largest component of this group, growing from 63,697 in 1940 to 235,436 in 1970 and 586,000 in 1999. The number of Black physicians and surgeons grew from 3,524 to 6,106 between 1940 and 1970, to 41,000 in 1999. See the following Table.

Table 2

Changes in Occupational Profile, Selected Occupations Number of Black Employed in 1000's (percent Black of All Employed in Occupations)								
Occupation	1940		1970		1983		1999	
Total Employed Civilians	45,166		77,309		100,834		133,488	
Total Blacks Employed	4,479	10	7,240	10	9,378	9.3	15,084	11.3	100.0
Managerial/Prof. Specialty	180	5	742	8	1,321	5.6	3,237	8.0	21.5
Executive, admin., managerial	45	1	148	3	506	4.7	1,488	7.6	9.9
Public officials/Administrators					35	8.3	92	14.0	0.6
Management-related occupations					172	5.8	478	9.8	3.2
Professional specialty	135	4	594	5	820	6.4	1,754	8.4	11.6
Engineers					42	2.7	95	4.6	0.6
Physicians	3.5	1	6.1	2	17	3.2	41	5.7	0.3
Registered nurses					92	6.7	204	9.6	1.4
Teachers, college/university					27	4.4	64	6.5	0.4
Teachers, except college/university	63	6	235	8	306	9.1	522	9.9	3.5
Lawyers and judges	1	1	4	1	18	2.7	50	5.2	0.3
Social workers					74	18.2	187	24.2	1.3
Clergy	17	13	13	6	14	4.9	36	10.3	0.2
Writer/artists/entertainers/athletes					74	4.8	162	6.6	1.1
Actors and directors					4	6.6	14	10.7	0.1

Athletes					5	9.4	21	19.0	0.1
Technical sales Admin Support	20	11	1,038	20	2,378	7.6	4,359	11.2	28.9
Technical & related support					250	8.2	466	10.7	3.1
Sales occupations					555	4.7	1,402	8.7	9.3
Administrative support					1,574	9.6	2,490	13.5	16.5
Mail and message distributing					144	18.1	209	21.1	1.4
Service occupation, Private households	1,523	27	1,805	20	2,300	16.6	3,278	8.3	21.7
	985	48	519	48	272	27.8	125	15.1	0.8
Protective Services					227	13.6	483	19.8	3.2
Services Private/protective					1,792	16.0	2,665	8.2	17.8
Production ... craft/repair	1,254	8	1,657	11	838	6.8	1,167	8.0	7.7
Operators fabricators/laborers					2,252	14.0	2,852	5.7	18.9
Farming/forestry/fishing					278	7.5	171	5.0	1.1
Farm workers	1,433	18	222	8	133	11.6	41	5.4	0.3

Source: United States Census Bureau, 2000. The numbers in the second column to the right represent the percentage of African Americans employed in this area.

The data in Table 2 is adopted from the Census Bureau's current population surveys, which reveal much about what has changed and what has not. Between 1940 and 1999, there were dramatic increases in absolute numbers and in the proportion of Blacks employed in certain occupations. But while these were substantial increases in absolute terms, they only increased the proportion of teachers who were Black from 6 percent of all teachers to 9.9 percent of all teachers, and the proportion of physicians and surgeons from 1 percent to 5.7 percent of all physicians and surgeons, compared with the proportion that Blacks occupy among all employees (11.3 percent in 1999).

In fact, certain racial and ethnic groups were unequally represented even in the medical professions. In 1998, Leon Bouvier indicated in his article "Doctors and Nurses: A Demographic Profile" that 80.5 percent of all U.S. physicians were non-Hispanic Whites—granted that non-Hispanic Whites comprised about 75 percent of the U.S. population. In 1990, there were about 13 million Blacks and 9.7 million Hispanics in the United States.[98] Additionally, a Pew Research report documents that "the 2010 census counted 50.5 million Hispanics in the United States, making up 16.3 percent of the total population. The nation's Latino population, which was 35.3 million in 2000, grew 43 percent over the decade. The Hispanic population also accounted for most of the nation's growth—56 percent—from 2000 to 2010. Among children ages seventeen and younger, there were 17.1 million Latinos, or 23.1 percent of this age group, according to an analysis by the Pew Hispanic Center, a project of the Pew Research Center. The number of Latino children grew 39 percent over the decade. In 2000, there were 12.3 million Hispanic children, who were 17.1 percent of the population under age eighteen."[99]

The shift in occupations was profound throughout the Black workforce. Whereas in 1940 only 6 percent of Blacks who were employed held positions in managerial, professional, technical, sales, or administrative support occupations, by 1999 just more than half (50.4 percent) were so employed. Conversely, the 1940 Black workforce was mostly (94 percent) employed in service occupations (principally private household workers and farm workers). Note that by 1999, about half that proportion, that is only 49.6 percent, were employed.

Some occupations became predominantly Hispanic as Blacks left them. An example is the farm worker category. The number of Hispanics employed as farm workers grew in the period 1983–99 from 182,000 (15.9 percent of all farm workers) to 348,000 (46 percent of all farm workers). During the same period, the number of Black farm workers dropped by more than two-thirds, from 133,000 to 41,000. The total number of Hispanics employed grew by 157 percent from 5,344,000 in 1983 to 13,747,000 in 1999.[100]

[98] For a detailed discussion, see Leon F. Bouvier and David Simcox, "Foreign-Born Professionals in the United States," Center for Immigration Studies, 1994.

[99] "Hispanics Account for More than Half of Nation's Growth in Past Decade: Census 2010: Fifty Million Latinos," a report by Jeffrey S. Passel, D'vera Cohn, and Mark Hugo Lopez, published by the Pew Research Center on March 24, 2011.

[100] United States Census Bureau, Community Survey, 2000. https://www.census.gov/hhes/www/poverty/publications/pubs-acs.html.

As published recently in the *Harvard* magazine, workers from all racial and ethnic backgrounds who hold jobs in the most vulnerable occupational sectors have been affected: they face working reduced hours, taking a lower-paid position, or leaving the workforce permanently. This is particularly true for Black and Latino workers, especially from disadvantaged backgrounds, who must contend with other unique circumstances that seriously curtail their ability to compete for good jobs. In fact, the same report also shows that Blacks and Hispanics and other ethnic minorities are concentrated and "clustered in manufacturing and low-paying service jobs and are therefore disproportionately exposed to unstable employment during economic downturns."[101]

The authors suggests that "these structural and institutional conditions undoubtedly contributed to the disproportionate rates of unemployment that Black and Latino males have experienced, compared to White men, since the mid-1970s."[102]

Against the backdrop of continued employment, income, and educational disparities, it is interesting to contemplate results of the National Educational Longitudinal Study, 1988. Tenth-graders were asked as part of the survey what occupation they expected to have at age thirty. The answers of Black and White children were strikingly similar: 50.3 percent of Black children expected to have a managerial, business, or professional position, while 45.3 percent of White children gave that answer. Both responses roughly approximate the proportion of occupations in the economy in those categories.[103]

The story is much different today. In fact, there is significant uneasiness and uncertainty about career and occupational options by minorities. In 2012, Kathryn M. Pond wrote a thesis at Georgetown University in Washington, D.C., titled "What's Wrong with I Don't Know? An Analysis of the Characteristics and Experiences of High School Students with Career Uncertainty," in which she concluded, "A

---

[101] James M. Quane, William Julius Wilson, and Jackelyn Hwang. "The Urban Jobs Crisis: Paths toward Employment for Low-Income Blacks and Latinos," the *Harvard* magazine, May-June 2013.

[102] Ibid.

[103] National Education Longitudinal Study, 1988 (ICPSR 9389) RSS Principal Investigator(s): United States Department of Education, National Center for Education Statistics.

student's race and gender play a role in the odds of being uncertain, as does the student's socioeconomic status."[104]

Unemployment

From 1948 to 1975, the ratio of Black and other races' unemployment to White unemployment fluctuated between 1.6 and 2.3 percent as the overall levels of unemployment rose and fell. Between 1980 and 1999, the ratio of Black to White unemployment fluctuated between 2.1 and 2.4 percent. Ratios for the latter period are higher because they exclude Hispanics and Asians, both of whom have lower unemployment rates than do Blacks.[105]

The 1960s and the period immediately following the Civil Rights Movement in the United States could be seen as the era for hope and increased expectation for social mobility and economic empowerment for African Americans. While strides have been made in areas of political inclusion and public policy to address disparities (albeit at a miniscule level), the unemployment rate for African Americans has not improved. With the increasing Hispanic population, the unemployment rate for Blacks remains noncompetitive. In 2013, the Pew Research Center published a report contending that "the widest gaps, when Black unemployment was as much as 2.77 times that of White unemployment, came in the late 1980s as the manufacturing sectors that employed disproportionate shares of African Americans shriveled. The smallest gaps, ironically, came in the summer of 2009 during the Great Recession; White unemployment rose so high, so fast, that the Black jobless rate was 'only' 1.67 times higher."[106]

Today, the Bureau of Labor Statistics estimates the unemployment rate for Blacks to be 13.4 percent compared to 6.7 percent for Whites. This type of alarming statistic caused Charles Krauthammer to write

---

[104]   Kathryn M. Pond's thoroughly documented thesis was submitted to the faculty of the Graduate School of Arts and Sciences of Georgetown University, Washington, D.C., in partial fulfillment of the requirements for the degree of master of public policy, p. 55.

[105]   Bureau of Labor Statistics, 2000.

[106]   Drew Desilver. "Black Unemployment Rate Is Consistently Twice that of Whites," August 25, 2013, Pew Research Center.

that the "tragedy of Civil Rights movement is it left people living in that age."[107] This is the postmortem of Jim Crow. There is no surprise then that the Urban League would document and the Black Youth Project would report that the Black youth unemployment rates in cities like Chicago is 93 and 83 percent nationally. It appears that while Blacks have made progress by forcing the government to change repressive laws and open the voting booths to all Americans who meet the constitutional age definition, the fight is not over. Discrimination, and unequal treatment, opportunity, and other social issues still plague Blacks in the United States. It is too early to celebrate the death of Jim Crow because the postmortem results are still inconclusive.

Assets

Asset formation, usually viewed as key to long-term financial success, has been severely limited among Blacks due to decades-old and continuing income differences between Whites and Blacks. Asian Americans have not suffered in recent years from such differences. In fact, median income among Asian Americans was 12-28 percent higher than that of White families in the period 1988–93. In 2012, the median income for Asians eighteen and older was $66,000 compared to $49,000 for the rest of America. During the same period, the Black median household income was $33,460, which was lower than the rest of America.

In analyzing Black versus White assets and wealth in 2010, Drew Desilver of the Pew Research Center indicated that the average U.S. assets for 2010 were $783,224 for Whites, compared with $154,285 for Blacks. The calculations took into account such assets as residential property, business equity, and primary residence. Additionally, the average household debt was $113,598 for Whites and $53,199 for Blacks. The average debt configuration included credit cards, student loans, real estate, and other loans. However, the Pew report concluded that "overall, though, Blacks continue to carry more debt relative to their household assets than do Whites: 34.5 percent of average assets

---

[107]   Documented in Real Clear Politics by Charles Krauthammer,
http://www.realclearpolitics.com/video/2013/08/28/krauthammer, retrieved
May 28, 2013.

versus 14.5 percent for White households."[108] Hispanics have not fared better than Blacks in their search for wealth. "The median household wealth among Hispanics fell from $18,359 in 2005 to $6,325 in 2009. The percentage drop—66 percent—was the largest among all racial and ethnic groups, according to a new report by the Pew Research Center's Social and Demographic Trends project."[109]

African American-Owned Business

"Blacks owned 823,499 non-farm businesses in 1997, employing 718,341 persons and generating $71.2 billion in business revenues. They accounted for 4 percent of the 20.8 million non-farm businesses in the United States, 0.7 percent of their employment and 0.4 percent of their receipts."[110] During the period 1992-97, the number of Black businesses grew 25.7 percent, or about four times as fast as all businesses (6.8 percent), but revenues grew more slowly (32.5 percent) for all businesses, which grew at a rate of 40.2 percent. Most (89.5 percent) Black-owned businesses were organized as individual proprietorships, the most informal type of organization, while only 5.2 percent were organized as C corporations, generally the most formalized type. Of U.S. firms, in contrast, 72.6 percent were individual proprietorships and 11.4 percent were C corporations. Subsequently, between 2002 and 2007, Black-owned businesses in the United States increased by 60.5 percent, totaling 1.9 million firms with 94 percent of those classified as sole proprietorship without any paid employees. In 2007, about 50 percent of Black-owned businesses were in the service industry, making up 115 with transportation and warehousing as the fourth-largest holding, accounting for 9 percent of all Black companies. But despite Black-owned businesses making up 7 percent of U.S. businesses, they

---

[108] Drew Desilver. "Black incomes are up, but wealth isn't," Pew Research Center, August 30, 2013. Published as FactTank.

[109] Rakesh Kochhar, Richard Fry, and Paul Taylor. "Hispanic Household Wealth Fell by 66 Percent from 2005 to 2009: The Toll of the Great Recession." Published as part of the Pew Research Center Social and Demographic Trends project on July 26, 2011.

[110] Survey of Minority-Owned Business Enterprises, Census Bureau, 1997 Economic Census.

generated fewer than half a percentage point of all U.S. business revenues. Of the 1.9 million Black-owned businesses in 2007, 13 percent had paid employees, which is an increase from 2002. These businesses employed 22.2 percent, with a total payroll of about $24 billion and increase of 36.3 percent. The top-earning industries in Black-owned businesses were in information, transportation, warehousing, and wholesale trade sectors accounting for more than $50 billion in receipts.[111]

Black-owned businesses are smaller in revenues, capitalization, profits, employees, and sales than are businesses as a whole. In other words, these Black businesses have less staying power through bad times, and their ability to invest in expansion and diversification is much more limited than is true of larger businesses. Consequently, they are less desirable borrowers than are businesses with more resources.

Environmental Factors

Black-owned businesses tend to be quite local in operations and dependent on the Black community for customers. This is a less-than-ideal base for business, given the pervasive poverty in the Black community. Many Blacks avoid patronizing Black businesses and professionals (physicians, attorneys) in the belief that they get more for their money in a White establishment.

Mass Merchandising and the Superstore

Small businesses strive best in neighborhoods where there is a long history of family ownership. The customer base develops based on trust and earnings, and capital is reinvested in the neighborhood. This has been the historical premise for the survival of small Black businesses. Recently, in retail operations, any small business, whether Black- or White-owned, finds it virtually impossible to compete with the market leverage of large chain operations, especially Walmart. These large retail chains are currently forcing some major retailers to trim their operations and outlets, as many broadened their product line to include a full grocery selection, and, as these companies rapidly grow, increased their number of outlets.

---

[111]   US Census 2011 ACS, Blackdemographics.com, retrieved on May 26, 2014.

Competition under such circumstances further weakens small and family-owned businesses, exacerbates the primacy of economy of scale, and centralizes and extends the rule of price competition. While this is the case also for White-owned small businesses, the ease in accessing capital makes it convenient for Whites to compete or bounce back from any market setback as compared to Black-owned retail units.

Economic Development

Population concentration in the cities, a major trend in the United States during the twentieth century, tended to create barriers to economic development by Black entrepreneurs and significant economic growth in most Black communities. During the 1930s and '40s, Blacks moved in massive numbers from communities in the Deep Southern states still afflicted by traditional racial patterns to metropolitan areas in other regions of the United States. The Black population became, to a much greater extent than before, a population housed in crowded inner cities with ever larger urban racial ghettoes.

Meanwhile, the rural and small-town communities left behind in the migration to the north was weaker economically. Often the migration included young, relatively well-educated Blacks who saw little opportunity for them in the traditional South and left hoping for success in Atlanta, Chicago, New York, Washington, D.C., Dallas, Houston, St. Louis, Los Angeles, Philadelphia, Boston, and Detroit.

While thousands of Blacks found relative success in unionized factory and construction jobs, office work, and professional occupations, most found themselves at the bottom of a larger, impersonal economic ladder. The cities offered higher costs of living to match the higher incomes. While they had grown up with personalized discrimination in the South, they were now faced with impersonal, institutionalized discrimination structured by job qualifications, bureaucratic procedures, and bank-lending policies operated by lower-level personnel in large organizations whose executives were normally inaccessible to an individual complainant.

Economic development in the inner city is hampered by fear of crime, low levels of disposable income, perceived lack of competent labor force, and the potential of falling real estate values. Economic development in rural areas and small towns is hampered by their tiny population bases, inefficiencies imposed by distance, lack of disposable income, inadequate public services and infrastructure (especially public schools), and often a group of community leaders fearful that development would diminish their ability to dominate community life. Racial discrimination is more subtle now, based on corporate and social systems rather than personal power. The all-powerful (White) high sheriff of Southern legend and fact is now replaced by a mixed-race police force trained to anticipate trouble and profile citizens based on ethnicity, age, and other presumed risk factors.

A sizeable informal economy exists side by side with the corporate economy, based on mutual aid within informal networks of extended family and friends. Although job opportunities may be better in large cities than in small towns, informal support systems are often more tenuous, based not on an extended family or on lifelong friendship but on more fragile relationships between recent neighbors or co-workers. It is probably more expensive to be poor in a big city than in the small towns from which many African Americans come. African American communities suffer from a continuing epidemic of broken lives characterized by disability, family breakdown, school failure, unsteady employment, poverty-level wages, periodic financial disasters occasioned by illness, family or gang violence, arrest and imprisonment, and other everyday disasters.

Educational attainment vital to success in the job market is often made difficult by negative teachers who are responding to their own pain and frustration in a school system that now seems to be producing poorly educated youth. Some students are branded early in their schooling as ignoring potential because they come from low-income or single-parent families that do not have the resources, time, or inclination to encourage their children in school.

Poverty

Personal income and poverty rates are not only determinants of family resources; they are central facts that define a community's ability to support Black-owned businesses, generate sufficient tax revenue to support schools and public services, and support features that improve quality of life. It is apparent that despite the assumed economic gains by Blacks after the enactment of the Civil Rights Act of 1965, progress in the areas of employment and income has been relatively slow.

During the thirty-five years since President Lyndon Johnson announced the war on poverty, the numbers and proportion of poor people in the population dropped significantly. The poverty among Black families dropped from 53.3 percent in 1959 to 29.5 percent in 1974, 26.4 percent in 1995 and 24.9 percent in 2000. Whites, on the other hand, have had much lower rates of poverty, even though their numbers are larger because they constitute 80 percent of the total population. The rate of poverty among Whites dropped by about one-half, from 18.1 percent (one-third of the Black rate) in 1959 to 8.9 percent in 1974 (again one-third of the Black rate) to 8.5 percent in 1995 and 9.1 percent in 2000. (Figures from decennial census of years mentioned.)

In 2001, poverty rates among Blacks and Whites were nearest parity in the Western states, where 13.7 percent of Blacks and 12.0 percent of Whites were poor, compared with 10 percent of Asians and 20.8 percent of Hispanics. The greatest regional imbalance of poverty rates is in the Midwest, where 25 percent of Blacks and 7.4 percent of Whites are below the poverty line, a ratio of 3.4 to 1. In this region, the overall poverty rates are lowest, at 9.4 percent.

The cumulative impact of income differentials is as great as or greater than the current impact. In 1992, only 26 percent of Black elderly had income from assets, while 76 percent of White elderly had such income. The differential in pension income was also considerable: 48 percent of Whites had such income while only 26 percent of Blacks did. The very poorest Black elderly had Social Supplemental Income (SSI) to offset poverty in 21 percent of elderly households, while only 5 percent of elderly Whites were poor enough to qualify for this income supplement.[112]

In the 2014 economy, the share of the population below the poverty line is $21,203 for a family of four, which is insufficient in today's economic for meeting basic needs. The poverty rate increased across the board in 2008; the poverty threshold increased exponentially as an outcome of initial recession trend. Poverty rates among African Americans and Hispanics more than double the percentage of White

---

[112] "Growing Unequal? Income Distribution and Poverty in OECD Countries," 2008, http://www.keepeek.com/Digital-Asset-Management/oecd/social-issues-migration-health/growing-unequal_9789264044197-en#page1.

Americans and Asian Americans. About 9 percent of Whites and 11.6 percent of Asian Americans live in poverty, while 24.7 percent of African Americans and 23.2 percent of Latinos are below the poverty line. The data also shows that little has changed in the last eight years. "African Americans' poverty rate is 2.2 percentage points higher than it was in 2000. For Hispanics, the rate is 1.7 percentage points higher. Whites and Asian Americans have seen 1.2 and 1.4 percentage point increases, respectively."[113]

Poverty in America can have a devastating impact on children. Home life is often chaotic, disrupted by parents' domestic discord or financial hardship or sometimes violence and jail. Older siblings and acquaintances from the neighborhood may glorify the sale and use of drugs, leading younger children to experiment with the excitement and "pain relief" that drugs can offer. Sometimes selling marijuana provides an important part of a family's income and is often tolerated by adults for that reason.

With regard to the majority of Black families with one parent, the assumption is the single parent is almost always the mother; one may also assume that older boys may be the only real role models available to younger boys. Girls, lacking a father in the household, seeking affection and validation from males, often start experimenting with sex early in their teens and get pregnant. Without a proactive support program, pregnant and parenting teens usually quit school early.

Perhaps we should be surprised, given the insidious and pervasive pressure of being Black in America, that there are not more rebellious Black youths willing to risk jail or injury to express their frustration in destructive ways. But this should not be misconstrued to mean the acceptance of defeat. The truth of the matter is that stories have been told about several Black youths who mere maligned by the system as not having what it takes to succeed in America and who persevered and

---

[113]   Published by the Center for American Progress, http://www.americanprogress. org/. Retrieved May 27, 2014.

Author's note: This discussion should be understood within the broad area of business, economic development, and education. There appears to be a correlation between access to education and employment and the ability to transcend the poverty threshold. The National Center for Educational Statistics has documented in its economic and population trend reports that educational attainment contributes to future earnings and employment opportunities.

made a difference. We have heard of Michael Jordan being benched by his basketball coach in high school; Les Brown talks about being labeled as having attention deficit disorder (ADD); Bill Cosby reminds us about him being labeled as having a speech impairment, and the list goes on. These are exceptional contributing members of society who seem to transcend any label.

The Handwriting on the Wall

Henry Lewis Gates, Jr. picks up where W. E. B. Du Bois left off. In a brilliant and thought-provoking way, Gates documents the reasons why one-fifth of all African Americans still live below the poverty level, and why many African Americans still feel excluded in mainstream America, even with the perceived notion that many opportunities exist for African Americans. One would be ill-advised to argue with Gates about the prevalence of this social dynamic. The assessments of African American political, economic, and social inclusion in the mainstream as echoed by Gates is also held by many upper middle-class African Americans, many who have parenthetically "arrived" but with no place to go. The notion of the working poor ascribed to by the Bureau of Labor Statistics is still prevalent and even a dominant category today. In fact, three-fifths of all workers today are classified as working poor and, sadly, they work full time.

There is a clear relationship between the labor force and poverty. It is instructive and explanatory to close this chapter with Gates's captivating and challenging insight.[114] Gates' dialogues with "well-to-do" African Americans seem to debunk the sporadic assessment that class and race are exclusionary.

---

[114]   Henry L. Gates, Jr. (2004). *America Behind the Color Line: Dialogues with African Americans,* New York: Warner Books.

Chapter 10

KEEPING THE DREAM ALIVE

So far, an attempt has been made to curtail the use of theories and models in this book to describe the African American plight and/or progress in the United States. This does not in any stretch of the imagination suggest that prevailing theories and models are not relevant, because used in appropriate context, many do shed light in an explanatory way as to the "whys" of the African American condition; any are, therefore, descriptive, not prescriptive. While dynamic prescriptions for curing the ills in African American societies are evasive, they are nevertheless not farfetched. But while searching for workable solutions, any effective scholarship must resist the attempt of lumping African American problems into neatly defined categories and applying testable generalizations whether those concepts were drawn from African American experiences or not. For example, I contend that measures of racism, prejudice, discrimination, and other social maladies must be group-specific if they are to be meaningful.

Prospects for improving the lives of African Americans in inner cities or rural America, for example, must follow a line ascribed to by Goldsmith and Blakely. In their work *Separate Societies* (Temple University Press 1992), they present an economic analysis of the African American and minority life in the United States. But they brilliantly segment the analysis to highlight the relative importance of developmental and growth factors and patterns for separate racial groups. They stopped short of "racial profiling" in many instances. These authors apparently recognize that "racial segregation has nearly always been a dominant characteristic of American cities. In the last thirty years, it has been in many ways more, rather than less, pronounced."

But in searching for the truth, these authors understand the economic divide in America is intensifying, but "once we account for race and ethnicity, household demographics, and physical isolation, we have the basis for explaining most of the inequality of income that the statistic shows."[115]

It is along these explanations and explications that I find a clearly defined line of poverty among specific racial groups. In the analysis in previous chapters, poverty as a prevailing issue in the African American community has been firmly established. However, it appears that the African American political agenda for social change cannot be completely articulated if the cacophonies of voices that emerge from African American communities are silenced by self-imposing groups that purport to represent African American interests. Some wish to be recognized as the only architect of an acceptable African American growth agenda. When this happens, it fragments African American interest and feeds into the majority rationale that African Americans are not cohesive and conclusive about political, economic, and social needs. Assessments such as these are meant to be controversial and thought-provoking because these discrepancies must be resolved if we are to move forward and leave behind the historical rift between the Southern Christian Leadership Conference (SCLC) and the National Association for the Advancement of Colored People (NAACP) where the NAACP continues to contend that only one organization should speak for Blacks and that should be the NAACP. This rift which began in the late 1950s may still exist today.

Past practices may not be sufficient today when used as the primary means for moving an African American political, economic, or growth agenda. Controversies such as this explain why the picture is blurry

---

[115]   William Goldsmith and Edward Blakely (1992). *Separate Societies. Poverty and Inequality in US Cities (Conflicts in Urban & Regional Development)*, Philadelphia, PA: Temple University Press, 54, 97.

Author's Note: In 2002, I met Edward Blakely, then Dean of The New School & University, and School of Public Affairs in New York. I was on an accreditation site visit team for the National Association of Schools of Public Affairs and Administration. I was impressed with his scholarship on African American life in the United States. The book *Separate Societies*, when read in its entirety, presents a detailed economic/developmental analysis of poverty and inequality in the United States, and in many cases, the authors offer not only descriptive approaches but useful prescriptive forecasting as only economists of their caliber could.

as we documented evidence of our lack of progress in the past several chapters.

What is appreciable today includes a self-assessment by African American leadership groups and a serious consideration for change and structural adjustments not only in the various developmental approaches for growth but in issues that matter most today. Our priorities must be dynamic and constantly scrutinized and adjusted. When the playing field changes and they are called a different way, for example, we must be dynamic enough to adjust. This is often not the case. Many times we are left behind and play catch-up in an American social, political, and economic environment that is in constant flux and usually not winnable.

As political opinions change, so must the political agenda. We must constantly seek new frontiers for progress. After all, it was W. E. B. Du Bois who wrote in his stirring book *The Souls of Black Folks* that the "rising of a nation, the pressing forward of a social class means a bitter struggle, a hard and shrewd sickening battle with the world such as few of the more favored classes know or appreciate the struggle for African American progress is not temperamental or temporal; the issues must be brought to the forefront for a national action."[116]

---

[116]   W. E. B. Du Bois. *The Souls of Black Folk,* Chicago: A.C. McClurg & Co.; Cambridge University Press, John Wilson and Son, Cambridge, USA, 1903; Bartleby.com, 1999. www.bartleby.com/114/.

Author's note: On the launch of his groundbreaking 1903 treatise *The Souls of Black Folk,* W. E. B. Du Bois indicated that "the problem of the twentieth century is the problem of the color line"—a brilliant, thought-provoking discourse on the predicament of African Americans in the United States at the dawning of the twentieth century. Du Bois the activist explains the meaning of the emancipation. He provides his views on leadership and education for the Black race. I have admired his work for years, and his courage, determination, and discontent with the vestiges of inequality has been contagious. Even after reading his book, I was reintroduced to his social activist ideas at Atlanta University as a graduate student. There I learned about his work as a social critic and his push for the education of Black folks. I owe a lot of my intellectual growth on the subject of Black struggles and its polemics to Du Bois. He enlightened me earlier on about Black politics in the United States.

Both the educational system and the criminal justice system contribute to the waste of millions of young lives through educational failure and imprisonment. The evidence is most obvious among young Black males, who are most likely to fail in school, enter the labor force with the weakest skills, be unemployed or underemployed in the lowest-paying jobs, and be arrested and imprisoned for marijuana possession. The patterns described here represent not only personal tragedies for Black youths and their families but an expensive waste of human resources. Ultimately, we all pay the bill.

Given the entrenched interests present in the education and law enforcement industries, a widespread popular expression of concern would be required to change direction and institute new priorities and policies. Public debate in the first decade of the twenty-first century revolves around the federal policy called No Child Left Behind, an admirable sentiment. But in practice, the pressure exerted by this policy caused some school administrators to encourage teachers to "teach to the test" that measures student achievement rather than fosters a spirit of enquiry and love of learning. Administrators are "explaining" poor results by citing the poor and minority students who bring down the average scores. Counselors and principals in some schools are encouraged to expel students who perform poorly rather than help them do better.[117]

New prisons are being built to house an exploding inmate population as more and more youths and adults are sent to prison with long sentences for relatively minor offenses. In some states, such as Georgia, rural communities, desperate for new jobs and economic development, celebrate the construction of new prisons. Corporations gear up to build and even own and manage new facilities. Educational and therapeutic programs, once designed to rehabilitate prisoners, are cut back in favor of get-tough policies.

---

[117] Richard J. Murnane and John P. Papay. "Teachers' Views on No Child Left Behind: Support for the Principles, Concerns about the Practices," *Journal of Economic Perspectives,* Vol. 24, No. 3, Summer 2010, 151–66.

A rational educational policy would seek to promote programs that are capable of helping children succeed rather than assigning blame to poor and minority students and their families or punishing the school systems that house them. There is a need for demonstration projects to test innovative education programs that may help the children who fail to stay in school.

A rational criminal justice system would seek to prevent crime, promote even-handed law enforcement, find alternatives to imprisonment for minor offenders, reform sentencing laws to make them more equitable, and provide means for prisoners to change their lives so that when they re-enter society, they will be self-supporting.

The data presented in this book clearly indicate dramatic gains in some areas, such as increased employment in relatively high-paid occupations that require extensive education. However, the data on poverty, unemployment, median family income, Black-owned business, and personal asset formation all point to a continued tilt in the proverbial playing field. Between 1989 and 2000, the White income ratio increased by 7.3 percent of Blacks. "Moreover, about a third of Black (35 percent) and Hispanic (31 percent) households had zero or negative net worth in 2009, compared with 15 percent of White households. In 2005, the comparable shares had been 29 percent for Blacks, 23 percent for Hispanics and 11 percent for Whites."[118]

The continuous rapid increase in income and employment by Whites compared to Blacks and other minorities bring a sobering perspective to the highly visible and undeniably encouraging gains in the number and prominence of Black athletes, actors, entertainers, and public officials, as well as physicians, attorneys, and executives. The spectacular changes in some of these occupations suggest strongly that Blacks will take advantage of opportunities when the playing field becomes more level, even when years of strenuous training or education are the price of admission. But the majority of Black workers and their families still struggle with social and economic conditions that, whether consciously or not, penalize the children of those who inherited a blatantly discriminatory system fifty years ago.

---

[118] Rakesh Kochhar, Richard Fry, and Paul Taylor. "Wealth Gaps Rise to Record Highs between Whites, Blacks, Hispanics, Twenty-to-One," Pew Research: Social and Demographic Trends, July 26, 2011.

Bibliography

The American Almanac, Statistical Abstract of the United States: 1995–96, Austin, Texas: Hoover's, 1996, Table 180.

American College of Physicians (2013). Affordable Care Act/Access to Care. Philadelphia, PA.,

retrieved May 6, 2014.

American Medical Association, Physician Characteristics and Distribution in the United States, 1995–96, 34.

Blendon, Robert J. et al. "Voters and Health Reform in the 2008 Presidential Election." *New England Journal of Medicine* 359 (19): 2050–2061.doi:10.1056/NEJMsr0807717. PMID 18974307. Retrieved November 3, 2008.

Broyles, Susan G. "Integrated Post-Secondary Education Data System Glossary," Washington, D.C.: National Center for Educational Statistics, August 1995.

Coombs, Jan (2009). *The Rise and Fall of HMOs: An American Health-Care Revolution*. Madison: University of Wisconsin Press, 5–6.

Cornwell, Christopher M., David B. Mustard, and Deepa J. Sridhar. "The Enrollment Effects of Merit-Based Financial Aid: Evidence from Georgia's HOPE Scholarship." University of Georgia, 2001.

Dahl, Robert A. (1998). *On Democracy,* Connecticut: Yale University Press.

Derickson, Alan (2005). *Health Security for All: Dreams of Universal Health Care in America,* Baltimore: Johns Hopkins University Press.

Dynarski, Susan (2000). "Hope for Whom? Financial Aid for the Middle Class and Its Impact on College Attendance," *National Tax Journal*, Vol. III, No. 3.

"Economic Survey of the United States 2008: Health-Care Reform," Washington, D.C.: OECD. Retrieved January 22, 2009.

Falkson, Joseph L. (1980). "HMOs and the politics of health system reform." Chicago: *American Hospital Association*, December 9, 2008.

Hanushek, EA, JF Kain, and SG Rivkin. "Teachers, Schools, and Academic Achievement," National Bureau of Economic Research (NBER working Paper No. w6691), 1998.

Harriby, Alonzo L. "Progressivism: A Century of Change and Rebirth," *Progressivism and the New Democracy,* Sidney M. Milkis and Jerome M. Mileur, eds. University of Massachusetts Press, 1999.

Healy, Patrick. "HOPE Scholarships Transform the University of Georgia," *The Chronicle of Higher Education*, November 7, 1997.

Hickey, R., Jacob Hacker, Pete Stark. "News Conference: the Case for Public Plan Choice in National Health Reform," Washington, DC: Institute for America's Future, December 17, 2008. Retrieved April 2, 2009.

Hoffman, Beatrix. "Health-Care Reform and Social Movement in the United States," *American Journal of Public Health*, a3(1):75-85, 2003.

Kane, Thomas (1999). *The Price of Admission: Rethinking How Americans Pay for College*, Washington, DC: Brookings Institution. Institute of Medicine, the Nation's Physicians Workforce, National Academy Press, 17–18, 34.

Kohn, Susan. "317 Million Reasons to Love Obamacare," CNN opinion. March 31, 2014.

Leys, Tony. "Health Plans Pit Low-Cost versus Public Coverage," *The Des Moines Register*, A1. Retrieved September 29, 2008.

Long, Bridget T. (2003). "How do Financial Aid Policies Affect Colleges? The Institutional Impact of the Georgia HOPE Scholarship." Boston: Harvard Graduate School of Education and NBER.

McAulliff, Michael. "Americans Die Sooner but Have Best Health Care in the World," *Huffington Post*, March 2, 2013. Retrieved May 5, 2014.

Murray, John E. (2007). *Origins of American Health Insurance: A History of Industrial Sickness Funds.* New Haven, CT: Yale University Press.

National Center for Educational Statistics. "Condition of Education 2011," 2011.

Pew Health Professions Commission. "Shifting the Supply of Our Health Care Workforce," October 1995.

Poen, Monte M., ed. (1982). *Strictly Personal and Confidential: The Letters Harry Truman Never Mailed*, Boston, MA: Little, Brown, 96–97.

"Progressivism." *The Columbia Encyclopedia*, 6th ed. 2001–05. Retrieved November 18, 2006.

Root, Damon. "The Best Legal Arguments against Obamacare," *Reason* magazine, March 24, 2012.

Sparks, SD. "Study Finds Gaps Remain Large for Hispanics Students," *Education Week*, June 23, 2011.

Sultz, Harry A., and Kristina M. Young (2011). *Health Care USA: Understanding Its Organization and Delivery*, 7th ed. Sudbury, MA: Jones & Bartlett Learning, 35–37, 230–32.

Truman, Harry S. "Letter from Harry S. Truman to Ben Turoff," College Park, MD: National Archives and Records Administration, April 12, 1949. Retrieved December 2, 2011.

U.S. Department of Education, National Center for Educational Statistics, "Digest of Education Statistics," 2000.

Viadero, D. "Lags in Minority Achievement Defy Traditional Explanations," *Education Week*, March 22, 2000.

Vicini, J., and Jonathan Stempel. "Top court upholds health-care law in Obama triumph," *Reuters*, June 28, 2012.

Walker, Forrest A. (Winter 1979). "Americanism versus Sovietism: A Study of the Reaction to the Committee on the Costs of Medical Care," *Bulletin of the History of Medicine* 53 (4): PMID 397839, 489–504.

World Health Report (2000). Geneva: Switzerland Health Systems Improving Performance.

Michael E. Orok has more than twenty-six years of experience in higher education. He currently serves as the Dean of the School of Humanities and Social Sciences and Professor of Political Science at Virginia Union University in Richmond, Virginia. Formerly, he was the Dean of the School of Graduate Studies and Research at Tennessee State University; Associate Provost for Academic Affairs and Graduate Studies; Interim Dean of the School of Graduate Studies; tenured Professor of Political Science and Director of International Programs at Alabama A & M University (AAMU) in Huntsville, Alabama; and Department Chair and Special Assistant to the Vice President for Academic Affairs at Albany State University in Albany, Georgia, among his many academic and administrative positions.

He is the immediate former Vice President of the Council of Historically Black Graduate Schools (CHBGS), and a 2005 graduate of the Millennium Leadership Institute of the American Association of State Colleges and Universities. He is the founding president of the Southwest Georgia Chapter of the American Society for Public Administration and is listed as a lifetime member of the Cambridge "Who's Who" registry of executives, professionals, and entrepreneurs. He currently serves as the first vice president of the Conference of Minority Public Administrators (COMPA). He also holds membership in the American Society for Public Administration and is the recipient of the Sweeney Award from ICMA.

He has read and corrected more than three hundred master's-level and doctoral research papers. He serves on the editorial board of many professional journals. He has presented academic papers at national conferences and published many professional articles and book chapters. He is the principal consultant with the Orok Consulting Group, LLC, a minority public management, public policy, and academic consulting enterprise. Dr. Orok holds a B.A. in Political Science from Central State University (Ohio), an M.A. in Management and Supervision (Public Administration) from Central Michigan University, and a Ph.D. in Political Science from Atlanta University (now Clark Atlanta) in Georgia.